LUCID DREAMING

Accessing Your Inner Virtual Realities

Paul Devereux and Charla Devereux

DAILY GRAIL PUBLISHING

CONTENTS

Authors' Note

The original version of this book was published in 1998. This 2011 Daily Grail Publishing edition has substantially extended text and is a different edit. The status of lucid dreaming is much as it was when the original edition came out, except for some tentative laboratory and academic work concerning possible involvement of certain neurotransmitters and regional brain activity, none of which is of direct relevance here. We feel that this volume represents a particularly comprehensive single source on the subject for practical use.

Your Own Virtual Worlds

YOU enter the cinema. The lights dim and you put on your 3D glasses. They look deceptively like simple sunglasses. The film begins. Suddenly you are thrust into another world, a world with three-dimensional vision and sound. You are transported into a virtual reality, usually one of extreme fantasy, like the 2010 pioneer of modern 3D movie technology, *Avatar*. With the recent flood of 3D movies, and, increasingly, 3D television, this will happen more often to more people. In a similar vein, the dramatically effective virtual realities of computer games take their players out of their actual, physical worlds into cyber otherworlds. But in the way that audio and visual digital technologies are mimics of our natural senses, so too are these movie and cyber otherworlds merely technological versions of natural virtual realities we can access through our own minds. These are not mere pale acts of imagination, but altered states of consciousness, other realities so vivid and seemingly tangible that they make the fanciest digital technology fade in comparison. These inner virtual realities are far beyond simple dreams, but dreaming is the gateway through which they can be accessed.

A third of our life is spent asleep, and it has been calculated that in an average lifetime we experience about half a million dreams. Yet for most of us in modern societies that part of our existence is like a closed book. We might remember an occasional vivid dream, but usually our dreams are just vague, fragmented shadows that evaporate in our minds as soon as we open our eyes, or are extinguished by the raucous sound of our bedside alarm. Some people even believe that they do not dream at all. We take the loss of this part of our lives very calmly, but think how shocked we would be if we were suddenly told that a third of our lifespan was to be taken from us! Yet that is effectively what happens, especially in our modern culture, which does not place a very high value on dreams – not officially at any rate. One of the reasons for this loss is that dreaming represents a discontinuity in our mental lives: when awake we can barely remember any of our dreams, and when we are dreaming, we forget that we are not awake. It is as if a broad, dark river of forgetfulness, a moat of amnesia, separates the waking and dreaming parts of our lives. Yet we can reclaim the night-side of our existence by taking specific actions to increase the vividness of our dreams and make our recall of them much more effective. This book will enable anyone to do that, but it will also explain that such actions can be merely the prerequisite for achieving something much more remarkable – namely, *how to stay awake while we are having our dreams.*

LIVING OUR DREAMS

Train ourselves to be awake in our dreams? It sounds an utter paradox. Up until the late seventies, even most scientists studying sleep and dreaming dismissed the notion as nonsense. But as we shall learn, two enterprising dream researchers, Keith Hearne in England, and Stephen LaBerge in the United States, devised experiments that scientifically demonstrated that people can be fully conscious in a dream, while monitoring equipment shows them to be physiologically sound asleep. This remarkable mental state, in which a person becomes fully conscious inside a dream, is known as "lucid dreaming". This is the natural condition of virtual reality, in which a new, separate space now seemingly surrounds you. You stand in perfect three-dimensional surroundings that dazzle your vision. No matter however sophisticated and advanced virtual reality technology might be, it is puny compared with what is available to you in this state. This is because no artificial virtual reality technology can match the power of the human brain, the most complex object we know of in the universe. Even conservative estimates say that the brain has twenty billion cells, each of which has ten thousand connections or synapses. And you have one of the latest models of this biological computer inside your own head and ready to use. There is a galaxy, a whole cosmos, between your ears. You are free to explore the infinite variety of worlds inside your own mind. Not limited, pre-programmed cyber-scenery, but an inexhaustible range of vividly-coloured, three-dimensional scenes proliferating in endless configurations recreated from your own memories, dreams, and perceptions. You can walk, float, fly, jump, and your body feels as if it is physically moving in these ways through the mental scenery. You can touch and handle objects in your virtual worlds – the waxy texture of a leaf, the silky smoothness of a dream-lover's skin. Men, women and children can populate these virtual worlds of the mind who are no different in the reality of their appearance to people you meet in waking life. These are not stiff, jerkily-animated figures but seemingly living human beings and animals and, perhaps creatures from mythology and other worlds and dimensions. Some might even be friends or relatives who have died, now standing as if alive before you. You can talk; you can hear. You can smell, touch, taste. All your senses are seemingly active. You can roam freely among Earthly scenes or those of other planets, and even float through the cosmos itself. There are no limits.

This book exists to show you ways in which you can learn how to switch on this magical theatre we call the brain, and which we experience as the mind.

Dreaming Lucidly

Because a person experiencing a lucid dream is mentally awake and alert, capable of making choices and exerting wilful action, he or she is able to react to dream events in the same way as if they were happening in waking reality. All the senses have their lucid dream equivalents, and the sensation of free movement, often in the form of flying, is totally convincing. Surroundings in a lucid dream are seen in brilliant detail and clarity, with vibrant colours. It is not mere vivid dreaming, but a whole other mental reality in which we can draw on the deep wisdom of the mind. The veils of forgetfulness are torn asunder – even though the dreamer is asleep, even though the body's physical senses are closed to the outside world, the person can fully remember waking life while in the lucid dream state, and on opening one's eyes to waking reality everything that happened in that state can be recalled. One does not "awake" from a lucid dream, one merely switches mental channels from one form of perceptual reality to another.

A Natural Process

This revelatory state of consciousness can occur spontaneously, so it is obviously natural and essentially safe. But because lucid dreaming can be learned, one doesn't have to rely on its rare, chance occurrence. As with anything else, however, one has to be responsible and disciplined in order not to become psychologically dependent on it. Also, anyone who has everyday problems distinguishing between fantasy and reality, inner and outer states of consciousness, should avoid the deliberate practice of lucid dreaming. But for most people it is a wonderful and natural means of extending and deepening their experience of being human in a variety of ways. We will explore these at greater length later, but here we can note such benefits as using lucid dreams for problem-solving, for in this state one has direct access to the remarkable creative resources of the human mind. Lucid dreams also offer excellent opportunities to rehearse situations one may be about to confront in real life. Again, lucid dreaming can be used to seek peak, mystical experiences, possible means of psychophysical healing, and general self-development. Over and above all these benefits, of course, is the simple fact that lucid dreaming provides an opportunity for sheer fun, adventure and excitement. This is true for any lucid dreamer, but think what wonderful possibilities this remarkable mental state offers those confined to wheelchairs, and who are otherwise disabled or incapacitated.

This is the valuable, exciting topic of this book, which will provide you with important background knowledge together with the richest selection of practical techniques we believe to have ever been presented in one place to get you started on a road that can literally take you beyond your wildest dreams.

CHAPTER I

Our Understanding of Dreams

W E cannot truly understand lucid dreaming unless we have a grasp of dreaming itself, and to do that it is important we have at least a nodding acquaintance with the rich history of the beliefs, ideas and research that dreaming has provoked from distant times to the present day, and appreciate the mysteries it still presents us with.

Dreaming in Ancient Times

The earliest dream documentation we have comes from Mesopotamia (modern Iraq and parts of Iran, Syria and Turkey). The Sumerians of southern Mesopotamia left pictographic records of dreams dating to c.3100 B.C. Later, when they developed a form of writing called cuneiform, incised on clay tablets, they left more complete and detailed dream records. Almost twenty-five thousand cuneiform tablets dealing with dreams were unearthed from the royal library at Nineveh, owned by King Ashurbanipal, an Assyrian ruler of the seventh century B.C. These contained information from many earlier periods, including a fragmentary account of the Epic of Gilgamesh, a legendary Sumerian king who

The Mesopotamians had methods of dealing with bad
dreams which were thought to be able to cast their
effects into the dreamer's waking life. The sufferer of a
frightening dream would tell it to a lump of clay that had
been rubbed over his or her body. The clay would then be
thrown into water to dissolve and with it the influence of
the dream.

ruled from the city state of Uruk in the first half of the third
millennium B.C. The Epic of Gilgamesh chronicles the hero's
ultimately unsuccessful quest for immortality, and is full of
dream references. These early writings show a sophisticated
knowledge of the symbolic and metaphysical nature of dreams.
There are also indications of methods to enhance dreaming.

In addition to the Nineveh tablets, cuneiform clay cylinders
were found that told of the dreams of Gudea, a Sumerian king
who reigned c.2200 B.C. A detailed account is given in which
Gudea receives instructions through symbolic dreams from
gods and goddesses concerning the building of a temple. This
was typical of the Mesopotamian belief that kings, specifically,
had a dream 'hot-line' to the gods. One of Ashurbanipal's
priests had a dream on the eve of a battle against Elamite
invaders, in which the goddess Ishtar appeared and basically
instructed the king to relax – "eat food, drink wine, enjoy
music" – and raise praise to her, as she promised victory in the
following day's battle. And so it was.

Dreams were also important in ancient Jewish tradition.
American dream researcher Robert Van de Castle notes
that a psalm in the Old Testament informs that the Lord

"giveth unto his beloved in their sleep", and elsewhere God announces that "If anyone among you is a prophet...I will speak to him in a dream". The stories of Jacob and Daniel are, of course, well known. Jacob slept on a stone and dreamt of a ladder connecting earth and heaven, with angels ascending and descending, while receiving a prophetic announcement from God. The Babylonians considered the Jews as potent dream interpreters, and this is encapsulated in the story of Daniel who was called on to interpret the dreams of King Nebuchadnezzar. The Israelite correctly predicted the ruler's coming period of insanity, and gained political power by his dream-interpretation skills, as did Joseph, sold into slavery in Egypt, by accurately interpreting the Pharaoh's dream as foretelling of seven good and seven hard years in the kingdom. The *Talmud*, the collection of rabbinical literature embodying Jewish civil and ceremonial law and legend dating to the fifth century B.C. but including earlier material, contains over two hundred references to dreams. One recorded belief was that demons and the dead could cause dreams. A hairy goat-like demon could promote erotic dreams, as could another called Lilith, who appeared as a woman to male dreamers and as a man to females.

Like the Mesopotamians, the Egyptians felt that dreams could contain messages from the gods, and that royal personages were their most usual recipients. A classic example of this was the dream of Thutmose IV (c.1419-1386 B.C.). The god Hormakhu appeared in a dream to Thutmose, promising him riches and a united kingdom if he would remove the sand then covering the Sphinx. When he came to power, Thutmose did this and recorded his dream on a stela placed in front of the Sphinx, which can be seen to this day.

The Egyptians seem to have believed that dreams were caused by the *Ba* – spirit or soul – leaving the body during sleep, as it did permanently at death. The *Ba* was depicted as a bird or human-headed bird in ancient Egyptian art. Psychologist David Fontana observes that the Egyptians did much to systemise dream interpretation, especially in the Middle Kingdom (2040-1786 B.C.). The earliest collection of Egyptian dream material dates from this period, and is known as the Chester Beatty Papyrus. It tables one hundred and forty-three good dreams, indicated in black, and ninety-one bad ones, indicated in red. The interpretations show a familiarity with the symbolic aspects of dreams, and also of their punning nature. The papyrus additionally contains advice on how to protect against the possibly evil consequences of bad dreams, suggesting that the afflicted dreamer rub the face with herbs, beer and myrrh to remove any dream contagion, and offer an incantation to the goddess Isis.

There were numerous temples dedicated to Serapis, the Egyptian god of dreams, of which the one at Memphis, built c.3000 B.C., was particularly important. Professional dream interpreters or oracles were attached to such temples. A temple at Abusir, dedicated to Imhotep, contained an oracular dream cavern where a traveller a thousand years ago claimed to see a statue of Joseph, interpreter of the pharaoh's dream, and that the cave was where the pharaoh had originally incarcerated Joseph. The Israelite was able to interpret the dreams of his fellow inmates, and it was this that brought Joseph's abilities to the attention of the pharaoh.

The ancient Chinese, too, had a highly developed interest in dreams. Similar to the Egyptians, they believed that dreams were related to the impressions the *hun,* the spiritual soul,

> The section of the *T'ung Shu* dealing with dreams is called "Chou Kung's Book of Auspicious and Inauspicious Dreams". Chou Kung was an eleventh-century B.C. mathematician, thought also to have been involved with the creation of the *I Ching*, the divinatory 'Book of Changes'. Researcher Robert Van de Castle notes that in China the term "Mr. Chou" is still associated with dreaming. So, for example, if a student dozes off during a class, the teacher might awaken the miscreant with the question: "Have you been visiting Mr. Chou?"

received during its nightly sojourns in the land of the dead. The ancient Chinese almanac, the *T'ung Shu*, contains a section on dreams dating to 1020 B.C. It breaks down dream imagery into seven categories of symbols, along with their meanings for the dreamer, and, like the Egyptian dream chronicles, recognises the punning nature that dreams can sometimes exhibit.

The Taoist *Lie-tseu* categorised dreams variously as ordinary, terrifying, arising from thoughts entertained during the day and from the activities performed in the waking state, and dreams of happiness. Taoist philosophy, traditionally founded by Lao-tzu in the sixth century B.C., felt that the world of appearances was an illusory flux of dualities, or interacting yin (negative/feminine/ receptive) and yang (positive/masculine/ active) principles. Only the underlying, inherent and indescribably pure state of creation, the Tao, was real, because it contained, dissolved or transcended all dualities. It is no surprise, therefore, to learn that the *Lie-tseu* distinguished between imagery resulting from strong yin or yang forces operative within the dreamer. The attitude of the fourth-century B.C. Taoist philosopher Chuang-tzu to one of his dreams famously encapsulates this emphasis on illusion and duality. He dreamt that he was a butterfly happily fluttering along from blossom to blossom. When he awoke from this vivid and enchanting dream, he could not decide whether he was a butterfly dreaming he was a man, or was man dreaming he had been a butterfly.

Dreams figured significantly in the traditions of India, too. The *Vedas*, the sacred texts written between 1500-1000 B.C., recount favourable and unfavourable dreams. Hymns to the goddess Usas and purification rituals and activities were described that could help dispel the effects of bad dreams. Curiously, though, the *Vedas* held that dreams of certain kinds of negative imagery, such as violence and aggression, could indicate a positive outcome in the waking life of the dreamer. They also maintained that dreams at different times of the night had variable prophetic effect, so a dream early in the dreamer's sleep cycle would not come true for a year, while dreams shortly before waking were already in progress in the dreamer's life – in effect, that there was a hierarchy of problem solving by the dreaming mind. This surprisingly sophisticated approach is continued in the later *Upanishads* (early first millennium B.C.), where ideas concerning the effects of the desires of the dreamer and his or her psychological state on the production of certain dream imagery are proposed alongside other more typical traditional theories such as dreams resulting from the soul leaving the body during sleep and visiting distant but real places in this and the other world. "The Hindu belief that some symbols are universal while some are personal to the dreamer foreshadows the work of both Freud and Jung," David Fontana observes.

It was not only the ancient civilisations of the Middle East and Asia that saw dreaming as important. We know that Native American tribes and tribal societies worldwide incorporated dreaming into their religious life, and from what has survived of their literature and traditions we have learned that dreaming had a significant place in the ceremonial life of the pagan Celts as well. Their seers, the *filidh*, continuing the traditions of the earlier Druids, conducted augury or divination by being wrapped in the hide of a freshly-slain bull – often then placed by a waterfall, stream or other place thought to be frequented by spirits. As he slept, the spirits would visit the seer in his dreams, and tell him what he wanted to know – the fate of a family, the outcome of a battle, or whatever information was sought. This type of "bull dream" or *Tarbfeis* had political significance too, for it was central to the choosing of a new king. After representatives of the various clans involved had made a decision as to who the new king should be, the choice had to be verified by divination. A

Fig. 1: Waterfalls were favoured places for receiving special dreams in cultures as diverse as the ancient Celts or, even today, Amazonian Indians.

bull would be sacrificed and a broth made from it. While the others chanted over him, the seer would sleep on the beast's hide, and was expected to see the new king in a dream.

Dream Incubation

This kind of purposeful dreaming is known as incubation (from the Latin *incubare* - to lie down upon), also sometimes called 'temple sleep'. To incubate a dream, a person concentrates on the nature or purpose of any dreams to be sought, and uses procedures and aids that help invoke such dreams by 'fixing' the intent clearly in the mind as sleep commences. It was widely practiced in the ancient world, and is still performed in some societies to this day.

Although the Mesopotamians left little in the way of a direct record of dream incubation, there are indications that they did possess procedures for dream-seeking. References suggest that some ancient Jewish seers also practiced incubation by resorting to a grave or a sepulchral vault and spending the night there, in order that the spirit of the deceased would appear in a dream and offer information or guidance. The Egyptians certainly incubated dreams and did so in an organised way. The person seeking a dream would go to a special temple, recite specific prayers, fast, and perform rites and activities in order to have a dream that could yield desired information. Immediately before going to sleep, the dream candidate might invoke the help of suitable deities by writing their names on a piece of clean linen, then burning it. If it wasn't possible for the person to get to a dream temple, it could be arranged that a surrogate could seek a dream on their behalf!

Ancient China likewise had incubation temples, and these were apparently active up to the sixteenth century. They were often used to assist political and governmental processes: so VIPs visiting a city would be required to spend a night at such a temple before commencing meetings or entering

In old Japan, as in China, dream incubation was operated as a high-level state activity. The emperor would have a dream hall in his palace, containing a polished stone bed called a *kamudoko*. The emperor would sleep on this whenever he needed dream assistance to resolve some problem of state.

into negotiations, and government officials were expected to resort to such places periodically for insight to help guide their waking responsibilities.

The people who raised dream incubation to probably its greatest sophistication in the West were the ancient Greeks. The first recorded Greek dream book dates to the fifth century B.C., and was written by Antiphon, an Athenian statesman, though references to dreams occur in the earlier collection of oral stories traditionally ascribed to Homer. Dream interpretation, called *oneiromancy* by the Greeks (*oneiros* being the Greek word for dream), came to be considered an art of civilisation. The fifth-century B.C. general and statesman, Aristides, left the first dream diary known of in the West. The father of medicine, Hippocrates (c.460-357 B.C.), wrote an essay called *On Dreams*, in which he mixed a belief in prophetic dreams and astrological ideas with some perceptive psychological and physiological observations associated with dreams.

Incubation or temple sleep developed along with the rise of popularity in the fifth-century B.C. of the healing god, Aesculapius, son of Apollo. At least three hundred and twenty temples were dedicated to him throughout Greece, the first one in Athens, and the most important one at Epidaurus.

Fig. 2: An ancient Greek statue showing the healing god Aesculapius with his/
Serpent-entwined staff, the *caduceus*.

The ruins of Epidaurus are still to be seen. It became a major centre which was built up over a century or more. The complex contained temples dedicated respectively to Aesculapius and to his daughter Hygeia, a hotel, altars for votive offerings, a library, a stadium and dream cells or *abatons*. These were built next to an ancient sacred well (it is noteworthy that all the Aesculapian temples were built over springs of pure, fresh water). They were effectively what we would think of as health spas, so clean water and beautiful surroundings were doubtless helpful in restoring people to better health. But the focus was on healing achieved through the intercession of the god himself, accessed by means of dreams.

A person seeking healing would stay at the temple, undergoing a variety of purifications, such as abstaining from sexual intercourse, drinking and bathing in the temple waters, fasting, sacrificing, praying and reciting invocations. An inscription found at Epidaurus states: "You must be purified before entering the sanctuary. He who thinks holy thoughts becomes purified". A special diet would be adhered to. The temple environment was liberally filled with statues and carved reliefs showing Aesculapius and his daughters, and votive models of limbs, heads, genitalia and other body parts made from terracotta left with testimonial plaques by previous visitors who had experienced successful cures. It is thought that in some cases harmless snakes slid freely across the temple floors, recalling the fact that a snake entwined around a staff was the god's emblem, known as the *caduceus* (see Figure 2). This image is retained today in the modern symbol of the medical profession, and incredibly, even carved on the wooden handles of drums belonging to shamanic healers in Siberian tribes. The favoured creature used for sacrifice was a cockerel,

Fig. 3: Although the *abatons*, the dream cells, have long disappeared at the ruined Aesculapian temple at Corinth, some of the stone couches there still survive, such as this one being tried out here by one of the authors. It proved surprisingly comfortable!

another symbol associated with Aesculapius. So the temple environment constantly reinforced the presence of Aesculapius and the healing process, and the patient's mind was heavily focused on the job in hand. By the time supplicants came to take their healing sleep, therefore, the set and setting of the temple would have combined to create a powerful psychological state of expectation in them.

After taking a herbal infusion to aid in fostering dream-laden sleep, the person seeking the healing dream would lie on a special bed in one of the *abatons*. This might be draped with an animal skin – often that of a ram – echoing the practice of the Celtic seers. Although Epidaurus and most of the Aesculapian temples are now in an advanced state of ruin, the temple at Corinth still possesses some surviving stone beds (see Figure 3). The person fell asleep in the soft, mysterious light of flickering oil lamps. Vessels for burning scented herbs have been found, and this incense may well have contained psychoactive plants. It was hoped that a dream of the god or one of his daughters or symbolic associations would be experienced during the night. In the earlier days, the dream itself was thought to be therapeutic, but the Aesculapian temples furnished special helpers or *therapeutes* who would interpret supplicants' dreams for them, advising on the course of treatment indicated by the dream imagery. There is evidence

Contemporary records from the sleep temples tell of a range of cures, some sensible, others bizarre and seemingly miraculous. There was Heraieus of Mytilene: "He did not have a hair on his head, but a great deal on his chin. Being ashamed because he was laughed at by others, he slept in the shrine. And the god, anointing his head with a drug, made him grow hair". Another inscription tells us: "There came as a suppliant to the god a man who was so one-eyed that the other had only lids in which there was nothing ... Certain people in the temple laughed at his simplicity in thinking that he would see with an eye that was not there. Then a vision appeared to him as he slept; the god seemed to boil some medicine and, drawing apart the lids, to pour it in. When day came, he went out seeing with both eyes". Another plaque tells of a Cretan woman who "thanks Aesculapius the Saviour, having got a severe ulceration on her little finger and being cured when the god ordered her to apply an oyster shell burnt and powdered with rose salve and to anoint it with mallow mixed with olive oil. And so he cured her".

that the floors of *abatons* were sometimes covered in blood, suggesting that actual surgery may have been performed. The therapeutes also sometimes applied poultices and ointments to the afflicted parts, and in cases of ear and eye complaints, a temple snake would be used to lick the eyelids or ears. Judging by the numbers of votive offerings and testimonial inscriptions found by archaeologists excavating these sleep temples, a great many treatments seem to have been effective. (Some accounts in the testimonial inscriptions tell of miraculous cures, but it is more than likely that some of these plaques were made by priests as a form of advertising!)

The Romans absorbed the Greek science of dream incubation for healing, and dream temples have been found at the far edges of the Roman empire, like the ruined temple of Lydney in England, which was dedicated to a local god, Nodens, and was active up until the time the Romans left Britain in the fourth century A.D. Instead of snakes, though, this temple used dogs to lick patients' afflicted parts.

Fig. 4: Only the foundations of the dream temple at Lydney, Gloucestershire, England, are now to be seen. Like its Greek counterparts, Lydney temple was sited by a spring.

DREAMING AT THE DAWN OF HISTORY

In the second century A.D., Artemidorus of Daldis wrote the influential *Oneirocritica*, five volumes of dream studies which built on the knowledge of the subject held by the ancient world. In some regards, his work contained relatively advanced observations. "He identified the importance of the dreamer's personality in dream analysis, and observed the nature and frequency of sexual symbols," David Fontana writes in *The Secret Language of Dreams*. "In his formulation that a mirror represents the feminine to men and the masculine to women, he even anticipated the Jungian concepts of the *Anima* and *Animus*."

Artemidorus' book was translated into Arabic in 873 A.D. and stimulated attempts to classify dreams. The Islamic world already had a close relationship with dreaming because the Prophet himself, Mohammed, had used dreams as inspirational sources for both military and religious purposes. For example, the *Koran* tells of an angel coming to Mohammed in a dream, and leading him to Jerusalem on a silvery steed where he was transported to paradise, meeting Adam, Christ and the apostles, and being instructed by God. A statement in the *Koran* says that the study of dreams is "the prime science since the beginning of the world".

One of the most famous of early Islamic dream interpreters was Ibn Sirin (died 728 A.D.), and versions of his insights were published until the tenth century. In the following century, a major work on dreaming was written by ad-Dinawari. This was influenced by Artemidorus. *Tabir Namehs*, dream books, are found throughout the Arabic world, and though Muslims did not practice Greek-style incubation, desired dreams were

Much of the *Koran* was revealed to Mohammed in his dreams. Over several years, he would ask his disciples every morning about their dreams, tell them his own, and offer interpretations. Indeed, it was a dream had by one of his disciples that prompted Mohammed to institute *adhan*, the daily call for prayers from minarets.

sought by reciting special prayers during the day, a procedure known as *istikhara*.

A tenth-century Greek Christian who went by the pseudonym of Achmet drew on both Arabic and Byzantine Christian sources going back to the fourth century in order to compile his *Oneirocriticon*, which became another important work on dreaming during the early historical era. Achmet emphasised that the circumstances of the dreamer had to be taken into account in any dream interpretation – so the meaning of the same dream might differ if had by a king rather than by a peasant.

In the Christian world, the significance of dreams was gradually devalued as the centuries went by. Dreaming fared well at the outset, though, with the early Greek Church having a particularly positive attitude. Synesius of Cyrene wrote a fifth-century treatise which maintained that the soul was taken in dreams to a "superior region" where it could be in contact with true things. Synesius felt that dreams could show the way to hidden treasures, and confer the powers of poetry on a relatively ignorant man. (Synesius even claimed that gods appeared in his dreams and improved his writing style!) Dreams were similarly seen as divinely inspired by early western Christian figures such as St. Augustine. Tertullian, an ex-lawyer who became a priest in Rome in the third century, included dreaming in his *A Treatise on the Human Soul*. He considered that "Almost the greater part of mankind get their knowledge of God from dreams". He also saw dreams as sometimes being due to weather, astronomical conditions and other "actions of nature", and to ecstatic conditions of the soul. Although Tertullian considered dreaming to be essentially a gift of God, he nevertheless commented somewhat paradoxically that dreams "are afflicted on us mainly by demons". This was a hint of what was to come, but the rot really began to set in with the attitude of St. Jerome in the following, fourth, century.

A LONG, DARK NIGHT FOR DREAMS

Jerome was a scholarly man, and admired the work of pagan as well as Christian writers. But then he had a dream in which he was brought before an otherworldly judge and condemned for reading pagan works. He was flogged, and called out for mercy. In return for being spared more lashes of the whip, he promised never again to consult pagan works. Jerome paid great heed to his oath made in the dream, from which he awoke weeping and covered in bruises. This dream oath had its most serious effect when Jerome was asked by the Pope in 382 A.D. to translate the Bible into Latin, for he seems to have selectively mistranslated the Hebrew word for witchcraft, *anan*. Whenever the Hebrew text specifically criticised witchcraft, Jerome translated *anan* as meaning "observing dreams", though elsewhere he correctly translated it as "witchcraft". Jerome's "Vulgate" translation, which was the authoritative Latin form of the Bible up until the twentieth century, therefore had the effect of denouncing the interpretation of dreams and greatly coloured official Christian attitudes to dreaming in the West (eastern Christianity, following the Greek Bible, was less affected). One man's dream therefore echoed down the centuries.

Macrobius, a contemporary of St. Jerome, also wrote on dreams in his *Commentary on the Dream of Scipio*. He used a dream classification system that owed much to Artemidorus but he introduced two dark concepts – the nightmare (*insomnium*), and night apparitions (*phantasma*). "In the moment between wakefulness and slumber," Macrobius wrote, the dreamer sees "spectres rushing at him or wandering vaguely about." He included the categories of the *incubus*, a male demon which sexually afflicted female dreamers, and the *succubus*, a seductive female demon who haunted the dreams of men. Although such denizens of dreams had been noted before, such as Lilith in the *Talmud*, this was their first introduction into Christian literature. The *Commentary* was republished many times over succeeding centuries, and became possibly the best-known work on dreams in medieval Europe.

In the thirteenth century, after new recognition had been given to the Greek language and the literature of the ancient Greek philosophers, the Dominican theologian, Thomas Aquinas, adopted the Aristotelian philosophy which emphasised rationalism. Dreams, seen as issuing from the wilder shores of human experience, consequently had little place in Aristotle's worldview. According to him, they were unable to provide meaningful revelations, arising mainly from somatic (bodily) conditions. In his *Summa Theologica*, a text which was viewed as exceedingly authoritative right up to

Despite his warnings of demonic influence in dreams, St. Thomas Aquinas was not above making use of them himself. He had been having difficulty with a passage in his *Summa*, and several times had to abandon his attempted dictation to his scribes. Then, one day, he started dictating the problem passage with the utmost fluency. He explained to a surprised scribe that he had had a dream the previous night in which the saints Peter and Paul, no less, had told him how to handle the complex theological thoughts he was trying to commit to paper. So for St. Thomas Aquinas, it seems, it was a case of "do as I say, not do as I do".

modern times, Aquinas referred to passages of the Bible, falsely translated by Jerome, which warned against dream divination. Although he considered dreams could be caused variously by astrological conditions, daytime experiences, somatic causes and divine influences, he stressed the risk of invoking demons by the use of dreams.

Jerome, Macrobius and Aquinas provided the basis for the ensuing demon-haunted centuries the Christian church inflicted on western culture. The demonic view of dreams was given extra impetus in a number of ways. Catholic priests were bound by celibacy, and that doubtless played a part in the occurrence of sexual themes in dreams, thus encouraging a demonic view. "It would not be surprising if celibate priests frequently experienced seminal emission or 'pollution dreams'," Van de Castle has noted. The belief in sexual demons, in *incubus* and *succubus*, took firm hold. The Jesuit priest, Benedict Pererius, announced that "the devil is most always implicated in dreams" and indicated ways in which devilish dreams could be recognised. He warned that "the devil tries to pollute the bodies of sleeping men with impure dreams". The confessor of St. Theresa, Father Gracian, pointed out that some dreams "are evil, sent by the devil, and often show obscene images".

The protestants were no better in their opinion of dreams, either. Martin Luther, the founder of the Protestant reformation, saw demons everywhere, including in bed. It seems that he felt that sin and Satan were the "fathers of filthy dreams". In the 1500s, the Calvinist Gaspar Peucer considered the investigation of dreams to be dangerous, and felt that divine dreams were only received by Holy Patriarchs and prophets, not by the common folk.

The atmosphere of Christian authoritarianism, witch-hunting and the Inquisition was such that it was potentially dangerous to talk about one's dreams, let alone interpret them. At the official level, at least, dreams had been effectively banished.

The Emergence of Modern Dream Research

The Age of Reason finally dawned, dismissing the dark, fevered night of medieval demonology. Dreams had never gone away of course, and despite official religious disapproval, dream books, often based on the classifications of Artemidorus, circulated widely. But now it was possible to study the mystery of dreams free of religious beliefs and in a more scientific, enquiring manner.

Early in the seventeenth century, Rene Descartes had a series of dreams that helped him to crystallise a philosophy in which mind and body, the spiritual and physical, were to be seen as separate. This "Cartesian split" had an enormous philosophical impact, and dream research has proceeded embodying this conceptual divide, with some people seeking a physical basis for dreaming while others prefer a more spiritual or psychological approach. On the one hand there were people like the seventeenth-century Thomas Hobbes who saw dreams arising from "distempers" in the body. On the other, there was the Romantic School, which came into its own in the nineteenth century. The essayist William Hazlitt encouraged the oracular use of dreams, and referred to unconscious sensibilities as did other contemporary writers in Britain and Germany. The German scientist and mystic, Goethe, and the English mystical poet and artist William Blake (who claimed that he was taught to paint by a man in a dream), both emphasised the power of the imagination and resisted the rationalistic approach.

In 1814, Gotthilf von Schubert discussed the picture language used by dreams and the spontaneous use of symbols in them. In 1846, Carl Gustav Carus referred to the "realm of the unconscious" with reference to the life of the soul. His ideas prefigured those of Carl Jung concerning the "collective unconscious" many years later. An increasing recognition of the psychological role of dreams began to emerge. Karl Scherner listed what he saw as sexual symbols in dreams in an 1861 book, foreshadowing Freud. He suggested the penis could be represented in a dream by tower, a knife, and other objects, while the vagina might take the dream appearance of a flight of stairs or a slippery path.

The American sleep researcher, J. Allan Hobson, writes that by the middle of the nineteenth century there was a ferment of experimental enquiry into the brain and mind. This began to split out into three lines of approach: psychology, psychoanalysis and neurobiology. The neuro-physiological work was a "bottom up" approach, trying to understand the emerging physiological data concerning the brain as the basis of mental phenomena such as dreams, while the psychological study of dreaming, the "top down" approach, moved on apace. Two key figures in this latter development were the French researchers, Alfred Maury and the Marquis d'Hervey de Saint-Denys. Both in their separate ways made detailed and prolonged studies of their own dreams, and brought a measure of scientific exactitude to the subject that held the seeds of the dream laboratory work of the following century.

Maury published the results of his dream research in 1861. Knowing how usual it was to forget dreams on awakening, he used helpers who would awake him at specified times so that he would have immediate recall of his dreams or mental states in sleep. He became particularly intrigued with the sudden flashes of imagery that often appear at the onset of sleep. We call these "hypnogogic" images today. He found he could trigger certain images in the hypnogogic state by pressing his eyeballs to produces sensations of lights, now known as the phosphene or phosgene phenomenon. Anyone can try this for themselves, by gently pressing the closed eyes in a darkened room. This convinced him that dreams were initiated by signals from the sensory channels, perhaps combining with memory. But the idea that dream imagery could arise spontaneously within the brain itself seems to have eluded him.

The other great pioneer of rigorous self-examination of his dreams was Hervey Saint-Denys, who published his findings in 1867. His study of dreams had begun when he was only thirteen years of age, and he started recording his dreaming life in words and in drawings, eventually producing a long series of dream albums. He came to understand the nature of dreaming, observing its associative properties in which one image can spark off different trains of thoughts and other images. He wrote: "The dream shows us the scaffolding of the mental apparatus as one rarely perceives it in real life, the life of conscious thought". Most intriguingly, Saint-Denys's detailed studies led him to the discovery of lucid dreaming, and he became one of the most documented lucid dreamers of whom we have record. We will look at his work in greater detail in the next chapter.

There were numerous other dream workers crowding the latter part of the nineteenth century. Among them were the German researchers Strumpell, Wundt and Muller, who in various ways considered natural and random "entoptic" phenomena arising in the visual system, particularly the retina, as the basis of the imagery within dreams. G.T. Ladd, working at Yale University, similarly felt that dream images arise from what he called "ideo-retinal light".

Various other researchers looked to internal bodily conditions as promoting dream content, for it had long been noted that sick people had dreams reflecting their condition. So a person with lung disease, for instance, might awake from a dream involving sensations of suffocation. Other researchers concentrated more on dreaming's ability to apply a magnifying glass to a dreamer's psychological state. F.W. Hilderband felt that a person's wishes propelled the creative

Brain researchers identify a number of basic types of "entoptic" ("within vision") images which they call form constants. They are automatically produced in the visual cortex at the onset of trance experiences of many kinds, both natural and drug-induced (dreaming, lucid dreaming, the out-of-body and near-death experiences are all forms of trance or dissociated mental states). These form constants are generated in the brains of all people in all cultures, and include spirals, fortification patterns (especially common in migraine), nested curves, lattice patterns, grids and crystalline forms. Repetition and rotation of such basic forms is common. They are produced in the retina and the visual parts of the brain, and dance vividly before the entranced person's vision. What processes or mechanisms in the brain actually cause these patterns is not yet fully understood. As trance deepens, the geometric form constant patterns can turn into realistic imagery as the brain adds hallucinatory and memory content to them. So, for example, an entoptic zigzag line might turn into a writhing serpent.

processes of the dreaming mind. The English pioneer sex researcher, Havelock Ellis, noted the primitive and instinctual elements in dream content, a factor that James Sully, considered by some to be the true precursor of Freud, referred to as "regression".

And then, at the end of the century, came Freud himself.

FREUD AND JUNG

Harvard psychiatrist J. Allan Hobson contends that had dream research been able to continue without interruption from Maury and Saint-Denys to the present, "the scientific development of dream theory would have been a continuous line". But Freud's psychoanalytic dream theory was the interruption – an interruption that lasted half a century, and which remains influential to this day.

Freud began his career as a neurologist, but perhaps because of the slow development of scientific understanding of the physiology of the brain as the basis for mental phenomena he commenced his psychoanalytical approach. This arose because he had noted that his patients often referred to their dreams when talking freely about their symptoms. This gave him the idea that dreams might be a way of delving into the unconscious mind, the id, where he supposed deep and potentially dangerous primal urges, particularly sexual ones, resided. This material was unacceptable to the conscious mind, and Freud considered sexual conflicts to be at the root of neurosis or "hysteria", and what he termed the "psychopathology of everyday life", in which he included slips of the tongue ("Freudian slips") and momentary periods of being unable to remember something. The function of dreams as Freud saw them was to act as protectors of the conscious mind. They derived their energy from unconscious desires that have not been fulfilled in conscious life. Such primal urges from the id slipped into dream awareness but were there repressed or disguised, and thus prevented from erupting into conscious awareness in unabridged form. Dreams censored the raw stuff from the unconscious, thus allowing us to have undisturbed sleep. In this view, dreams are like security guards fending off marauders at the boundaries of our sleeping mind, which are far less secure than those surrounding our waking ego. The marauders were the "latent content" in a dream, while the imagery we could consciously recall from our dreams was the "manifest content" in which the unconscious material was condensed into complex, hybrid images or disguised by symbols, thus preventing it from entering the conscious sphere directly. The incoherence often produced by this process – called by Freud "dream work" – was subjected to "secondary revision" allowing the creation of a "dream facade" in which the jumbled elements could be woven into a connected story. Freud considered the ease with which dreams are forgotten, or fail to be recalled by the waking mind, to be a further element of the censorship function of dreaming. In short, dreams, according to Freud, sanitised, repressed and disguised unacceptable psychic content. He hit on the idea of analysing dreams and using free-association word techniques to get at the root of repressed tensions or conflicts causing a patient's neurosis. Thus was psychoanalysis born.

Freud published his *The Interpretation of Dreams* in 1900. Although it was eventually to prove enormously influential, it did not start out that way, selling only 351 copies in its first six years. But it went on to have many later editions, and it was translated into virtually all the major languages of the world. Freud founded the psychoanalytic school as a professional organisation, and it had its specialised method of training, its own journals and conferences. Despite the fact that *The Interpretation of Dreams* contained a useful index to dream literature, Freud tended to ignore or minimise the influence provided by the work of earlier and contemporary researchers who had also referred to the unconscious mind, dream symbolism, the process of repressing primitive desires, and who considered dreams to be instigated by wish fulfilment. Where he was obliged to acknowledge another's research, he did so in self-referential ways. One historian of science has commented that a "cult-like orthodoxy" built up around Freud's theories.

Because his theories did not adequately deal with all dream phenomena, Freud chopped and changed some of his ideas over the first decades of the twentieth century, but overall he left something of an unfortunate stain on dream research, for he considered dreams to be a form of "abnormal psychical phenomena" and to be of no practical importance. Some of his pupils eventually broke free from the narrowness of Freud's theories to develop broader views on the nature of dreams. None did so with greater effect than Carl Jung.

Jung was aware of the symbolic content of dreams, and accepted that unconscious material could play a part in neurosis and mental illness, but saw the imagery and themes recurring in so many patients' dreams, hallucinations and delusions as indicating material that was transpersonal, that is to say not always arising from an individual's personal conflicts but belonging to a larger body of collective and ancient imagery residing in the depths of the human psyche. Jung recognised that similar themes and images also occurred in world mythology and religious iconography. So he forged his idea of a "collective unconscious" and coined the term "archetype", referring to imagery or symbols directly generated – or "constellated" to use a Jungian term – by some primordial, myth-making part of the unconscious mind. To Jung, therefore, some of our more profound dreams can provide a portal through which the inherited deep processes of the unconscious mind are to be glimpsed and perhaps engaged with. He collided with Freud who considered sexuality as the prime unconscious force in dream and mental life; rather, Jung argued, sexual symbolism was often a facade for deeper, non-sexual spiritual meanings and psychic functions. Jung was concerned to probe the deeper meanings of symbols in dreams, exploring them in the transpersonal terms of world mythological and symbolic systems. Jung found alchemy to be one of the most powerful of such systems from a western viewpoint.

THE SLEEPING BRAIN

Psychoanalysis overshadowed much of mainstream scientific concern with dream research in the first part of the twentieth century, and eclipsed the earlier work of Saint-Denys and Maury, but the seeds were nevertheless being quietly laid for major breakthroughs in the physical, scientific study of dreams and the sleeping brain.

In 1914, the work of the French sleep scientist Nicholas Vaschide was published. He was amongst the first to make all-night observations of sleeping people. While he was impressed with Freud, Vaschide felt that the theory that dreams resulted from deep-seated wishes could not explain unpleasant dreams. So he took to the collection of observable data from sleeping subjects, monitoring their behaviour, respiration patterns and heart rate, and interrupting their sleep every so often to gain their reports of dreaming or whatever other current mental state they were experiencing. (He discovered that over eighty percent of his subjects could not recall their dreams unless he specifically awoke them during the night.) Vaschide noted that there was periodic motor activity accompanying dreaming – "the muscles have their own grammar". He observed tremors of the eyelids, changes in facial muscles, nasal dilation, periodic changes in vasoconstriction and vasodilation, and much more in sleepers. He also found that people seemed to dream in bouts and not continuously through the night. With these data, and his increasing conviction that sleep and dreaming were positive functions of the brain and not merely "idling" aspects of the waking consciousness at rest, he hovered on the brink of making the great discovery of modern dream research, namely, the cycles of Rapid Eye Movement (REM) or dreaming sleep. But it just eluded him, and the world still had to wait some decades for that breakthrough to occur.

The study of sleeping subjects became the key way in which those seeking physical data about sleep and dreaming proceeded. Contemporaries of Vaschide in America and Europe conducted their own, similar studies. Most researchers of this period were fascinated by apparent "motor" action in dreams like walking, running, swimming and flying, and the interaction between dreaming and bodily, physiological, changes. French psychiatrist Henri Beaunis was convinced that dreaming, like all mental states, depended on the physical states of the brain, and made studies of his own dreams. Italian scientist Sante de Sanctis observed sleeping dogs, and from distinctive movements of their muzzles and barking within sleep concluded that the animals dreamed just like human beings. But clear knowledge of how the brain functioned, let alone obtaining precise physical measurements from it, took many years to develop.

Spanish scientist and 1906 Nobel prizewinner, Ramon y Cajal, discovered the nature of the neuron or brain cell, allowing a cellular approach to the study of the brain, and making him the father of modern neurobiology. Over the same period, the awareness that the brain produces its own electricity became increasingly significant to researchers. In 1875, Richard Caton had been able to record wave activity in a rabbit's brain by applying a voltmeter to its surface, producing what is now called an electro-encephalogram – an EEG. But while it was known that brain cells were connected by wire-like fibres that conducted electricity, measuring the remarkable small and rapid pulses of energy with which neurons communicate with one another depended on the technological development of suitable monitoring equipment. A major breakthrough came in the 1930s with the invention of the oscilloscope at Cambridge. This allowed sensitive measurements of electrical brain activity and led to a tidal wave of new brain research. Insights into how the brain functioned were gained that had remained a closed book to Freud.

A range of sensitive measuring devices or polygraphs were developed so that brain and bodily processes could be monitored. The autonomous activity of the brain became more and more evident: it could activate itself, and did not rely solely on the input of sensory stimuli from the outside world. In dreaming, there is a blitz of self-generated activity in the brain which conjures the impression of the real world before the dreamer's inner eye.

A key finding was that of various wave frequencies that swept across the brain in various mental states. German psychiatrist Hans Berger, who in 1928 had successfully applied Caton's EEG approach to the human brain, noticed the appearance of an EEG rhythm of 8-12 cycles per second (Hertz or Hz) when his subjects closed their eyes in preparation for sleep. This has become known as the alpha rhythm. Berger measured the onset of high-voltage, slow-wave patterns as his subjects drifted deeper into sleep. In 1933, the oscilloscope was able to confirm these findings, and because of its sensitivity it brought brain rhythms into the arena of respectable scientific research. We now know that when we are awake with our eyes open we typically generate low-voltage, fast beta brain rhythms in the 12-18 Hz range, then we experience the alpha rhythms when our eyes are closed and we are in a relaxed but alert state. As sleep creeps up on us higher-voltage theta rhythms develop in the 4-8 Hz range. When we lose waking conscious altogether and are enfolded by sleep, the EEG trace shows a distinctive waveform known as the sleep spindle whose amplitude rises and falls at a frequency of 15-18 Hz. In deepest sleep, very high-voltage, slow 1-4 Hz delta waves dominate. Because EEG electrodes are placed on the scalp, it is still not known where exactly such electrical rhythms originate within the brain.

As the understanding of the brain's electrical activity developed, so too did the awareness of its chemical nature. It is the chemistry that mediates the electricity of the brain, making it an electrochemical organ. Chemicals such as serotonin and dopamine are just two of the many neurotransmitters that carry nerve impulses. Molecules of such substances are held in "buttons" at the ends of the nerve fibres extending from brain cells, and act as vehicles for communication across the gap or synapse between the end of a fibre and the membrane of the next, receiving neuron. Neurotransmitters all have specific effects, and their actions are switched off by the electrically-induced appearance of "antidote" chemicals.

Interestingly, a dream and dream incubation actually helped to extend the knowledge of brain chemistry. Otto Loewi, a Nobel prizewinner, was trying to understand why heart action slowed when he electrically stimulated the vagus nerve leading to the heart. He figured that the electrical pulse probably liberated a chemical which damped down the excitability of the cardiac muscle cells, but he couldn't think of an experiment to isolate the supposed chemical and so confirm his theory – at the time he was doing his work there were no means of measuring tiny amounts of substance in the blood. Then one night Loewi had a dream. He knew it had shown him a solution to the experimental difficulty, but he had forgotten its content! So the next night he went to sleep concentrating on having the dream again – simple dream incubation. When he awoke he remembered the required dream, and rushed to his laboratory to carry out its solution before he forgot it. He prepared two frogs. He electrically stimulated the vagus nerve of one, causing its heart to slow down. He then collected the blood from the frog's heart and administered it to the other creature. Its heart, too, slowed down as a result, thus proving that there had to be a chemical produced by the electrical stimulation of the first frog's vagus nerve that was present in its blood. The chemical was later identified as acetylcholine, and was found to be effective at many locations in the body where motor nerves excited skeletal muscles. It has also been possible to experimentally manipulate acetylcholine to produce REM sleep and dreaming.

The electrochemical activity of the brain can now be measured with considerable precision with new generations of monitoring equipment, but there is yet much to be learned.

THE MEASURE OF DREAMS

One of the most important discoveries of modern dream research took place in 1953, which, coupled with the developments in monitoring technology, has opened up whole new vistas on the dreaming process. As part of his research, Eugene Aserinsky, a medical student working in the "dream laboratory" of physiologist Nathaniel Kleitman at the University of Chicago, was observing sleeping infants. He noted that the infants' eyes moved beneath their closed lids for certain periods of time. He and Kleitman attached electrodes near the eyes of their tiny subjects and were able to more precisely monitor these rapid eye movements. This type of measurement is called an electrooculogram or EOG. Aserinsky and Kleitman quickly went on to confirm that adult sleepers showed similar patterns of rapid eye movements (REM). They suspected that the REM periods coincided with dreaming, and that they might be caused by the dreamer looking at activities taking place in the dream. When they awoke subjects during REM periods, most of them reported they were having a dream, while the majority of subjects reported no dreams when awoken from sleep exhibiting no rapid eye movements (NREM). Making other measurements, the Chicago dream researchers found that REMs were accompanied by slightly increased heartbeat and breathing rates and an EEG pattern showing low-voltage activity not usually expected during sleep. William Dement, another student who followed Aserinsky into Kleitman's lab, conducted more intensive monitoring of sleep cycles, and strengthened the association of REM periods with dreaming.

This work and subsequent research has combined to give us a fairly clear picture of the nature of a normal sleep cycle, when dreaming occurs in it, and what physiological events accompany it.

SLEEP CYCLES

In most sleep cycles we fall through four stages of NREM sleep, rise back to the first stage, when we might briefly experience REM sleep, then sink back down into NREM sleep, back up again to the first sleep stage or level, have a longer period of REM sleep, and so on through the night, rising and falling through NREM sleep as if traversing a series of valleys and ridges, with the REM interludes getting longer and longer, like ever-widening plateaux dividing the valleys of NREM sleep. To become proficient at lucid dreaming, it is exceedingly helpful to be familiar with this picture, which we can sketch in a little more detail here.

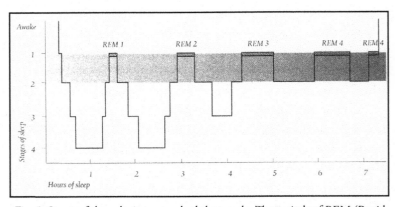

Fig. 5: Stages of sleep during a standard sleep cycle. The periods of REM (Rapid Eye Movement) sleep, in which most dreaming occurs, become longer toward the latter part of the cycle.

The beta rhythms of wakefulness are replaced by alpha rhythms as we close our eyes and settle down. As we fall asleep, we might experience fleeting images and dream fragments. These transient hypnogogic images tend not to be accompanied by the REMs that coincide with more vigorous, complex and prolonged dreaming periods, but as we shall learn in later chapters this can be a useful phase in which to attempt lucid dreaming. As we enter STAGE 1 sleep, the EEG shows a mixed bag of low-voltage brain frequencies, but there are no sleep spindles, "K-complexes" (sharp upward then downward patterns), or delta waves. Sleep spindles appear as we fall into STAGE 2 sleep, along with K-complexes. Delta rhythms increase in STAGE 3 and when they occupy more than half of the EEG tracing we have arrived at STAGE 4 sleep, the bottom of the NREM "valley". After an hour or so of this deep sleep, we climb back up to STAGE 1. REM activity is always associated with STAGE 1, and at this first return to STAGE 1 we might experience a few minutes of REMs and the EEG trace will often show a "saw-tooth" pattern. We then fall back down through the stages of NREM sleep, though as the night progresses, we sink less and less deeply, perhaps not even returning to STAGE 4. The STAGE 1 REM periods recur at approximately 90-minute intervals, becoming more prolonged each time – the final REM period of the sleep cycle might last anything from half an hour to an hour. This is another particularly useful time in the sleep cycle in which to attempt lucid dreaming.

Multi-channel polygraph measurements in dream laboratories have now provided detailed knowledge of the physiological changes that can accompany dreaming. The slow regular breathing of NREM sleep can be punctuated by rapid, shallow breathing during REM sleep. This and increased heart rates during REM sleep indicates excitation perhaps caused by emotional responses to dream situations (though there is a chicken and egg debate amongst experts as to whether the emotional arousal is caused by dream content or vice versa). Muscle tone, measured by an electromyogram or EMG, decreases during dreaming. This relaxation of most muscles along with reduced spinal reflexes during dreaming mean that the dreamer is effectively paralysed except for respiratory and eye muscles, and so cannot perform activities being dreamt of. Also during the REM state, urine volume and composition change, and genital arousal occurs. Men experience erections, and increased vaginal blood flow has been measured in women. Erotic dreams are not necessary for such arousal – rather, it is an automatic response to the neurological activity involved in dreaming sleep. There is significantly increased blood flow through the brain, also, during REM sleep.

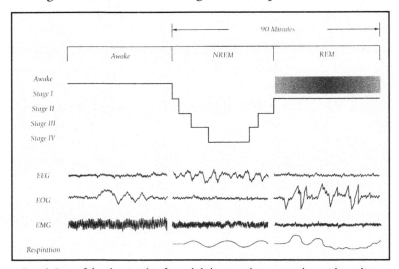

Fig. 6: Part of the sleep cycle of an adult human shown together with readings for EEG (measures electrical activity in the brain), EOG (measures rapid eye movements), EMG (measures muscle tone), and respiration.

EEG readings alone cannot indicate if a person is dreaming: concurrent eye movement and muscle tone measurements are also required.

Although REM sleep is equated with what most of us consider to be dreaming – hallucination-like mental events containing visual content, storylines, actions, and changes of scene – it would be wrong to think of NREM sleep as devoid of mental activity. Research indicates that dreaming still occurs, though it tends to be more thought-like and conceptual. In some people the differences between REM and NREM reports differ only a little. And it has already been noted that the early, hypnogogic stages of NREM sleep can contain rapid sequences of pictures (and also auditory effects). These tend not to have the complexity of full-blown dreams, however, and are sometimes termed "dreamlets". But the dreaming mind appears to be constantly active, even if the forms of that mentation vary.

DREAM MYSTERIES

It can be seen that dream research today consists of competing physical "brain" models and mental or psychological "mind" models. Some researchers consider dreams to be simply a rubbish disposal system getting rid of unwanted or excess impressions of the day, and that attempts to remember them actually interfere with such necessary mental processing. Others consider them a gateway to understanding the spiritual depths of the unconscious mind, while others deny the existence of an unconscious mind at all! There are those who feel that the interpretation of one's dreams can help an individual achieve psychological wholeness, while some researchers claim that dreams are just the unimportant, incoherent result of random firings of the brain's neuronal circuitry. There is a general feeling that a model needs to be found that encompasses both physical and mental approaches.

The contest between these polarised approaches becomes even more philosophically fraught when we consider the possibility of dreams containing paranormal elements. The most usual class of dreams to be reported of this type are precognitive or prophetic ones. Both Freud and Jung were confident that such dreams did occur. A classic example involved the assassination of Archduke Franz Ferdinand in 1914 – an event that triggered the First World War. Bishop Lanyi, the archduke's former tutor, foresaw the murder in a dream, and vainly tried to get a warning through to Ferdinand. The American president Abraham Lincoln dreamt of his own assassination! A few days before John Wilkes Booth murdered him, Lincoln found himself in a dream wandering around the White House and encountering a grieving group of people around a body that had its face covered. One of the mourners told him that it was the President, who had been killed by an assassin. The famous writer Mark Twain (Samuel Clemens) dreamt of seeing the corpse of his brother Henry laid out in a metal coffin. On its chest, the body had a bouquet of white flowers with a single red bloom. A few days afterwards, a Mississippi river boat exploded killing and injuring many passengers. Henry was one of the injured, and hung on several days before dying. When Mark Twain went to the temporary morgue in Memphis to see him, his body was in a metal coffin supported by two chairs. As Twain entered the room, so too did a woman carrying a bunch of white flowers, in the midst

Ron, an acquaintance of one of the present authors, underwent a remarkable case of precognitive dreaming in 1970. He became distressed due to dreams he had been having in each of which his deceased grandfather showed him a sheet of paper with a message on it. The word or words varied from night to night, but Ron, an avid horse fancier, soon realised they either were the names of horses running in various races, or were clear allusions to their names. Ron placed bets on the horses indicated in the dreams, and they all won. More than that, he shared his dream tips with co-workers. The group of friends was betting so successfully so often, in fact, that the local bookmaker got to the point of banning the men. But why was Ron so distressed? "Because I am too scared to go to sleep!" he replied. "I've become terrified that one of these nights my grandfather will hold up a message telling me of some future event – like my own death – that I don't want to know about." Eventually, the dreams simply stopped.

of which was one crimson rose. She laid the flowers on Henry's body, as she was one of the hospital workers who had been moved by the young man's vain struggle for life.

Inexplicable healing has also been associated with dreaming. Dream researcher Patricia Garfield cites the case of a woman who had suffered severe and debilitating migraine headaches for some forty years. Then one night she had a long and complex dream in which a man laid a hand on her head stating that she would never again experience a migraine headache. Up to the time of Garfield's recounting of the dream, the woman had, indeed, remained symptom-free. Van de Castle records the case of a physician suffering from recurring acute bronchitis. In a dream, his long-dead sister appeared to him saying, "We have come to cure you". As she vanished, the doctor felt a searing, electric-like shock in his brain which then spread down through his body. On awakening, he found himself free of bronchitis, and it did not subsequently recur.

Telepathy is another claimed paranormal faculty that seems to be effective during the dream-state. This was even subjected to experiment in a series of investigations at a dream laboratory in New York's Maimonides Medical Center. An "agent", physically isolated from the dreaming subject, would attempt to mentally transmit the image of a randomly selected art print to the sleeper. The subject would then be carefully checked to see if the image was incorporated in his or her dream. The rigorous and well-designed Maimonides experiments were highly successful, with positive correlations of over eighty percent being achieved.

MOVING ON

Quite apart from the possible paranormal potential of dreams, it is difficult to keep one's own dream journal for long without seeing the emergence of a distinct "dream intelligence" that can often perceive psychological and personal situations more clearly and honestly (and often more wittily!) than the waking mind, and is able to provide warnings, counselling and healing. Simplistic "waste disposal" and "random" theories of dreaming do not hold up well against this sort of direct experimentation, which is open to everyone, as is lucid dreaming, in which waking consciousness inhabits a dream. In this enterprise you can be as much at the cutting edge as any scientist – right there, seeing and learning just how consciousness works, and what weight can be placed on dreams and their interpretation, and perhaps being able to direct healing and paranormal aspects of your dreaming.

So now, armed with this background history of dreaming, the outline of modern research, and a basic understanding of the main theories, beliefs, knowledge and terminology regarding dreams, we can turn in an informed way to the closely related tasks of mastering our dreams and learning how to voyage fully conscious into the dreamworld.

CHAPTER 2

THE MIRACLE OF LUCID DREAMING

W AKE UP! That was the basic message of Tibetan dream yoga, the earliest and most comprehensive organised system for the development and practice of lucid dreaming we know of. The yogi had to become aware that all states of mind – whether dreaming, in trance, in the after-death *bardo* states, or waking consciousness – were illusion. Only the primordial, natural state of mind known as the Clear Light, or the Void, is reality. Lucid dreaming was included as one of the six yogas (or laws) by the tenth-century Indian Tantric Buddhist, Naropa. The first Tibetan to study under Naropa was called Marpa, and it is thought he brought the six yogas, and therefore dream yoga, into Tibet in the eleventh century, though some scholars claim there were active schools of dream yoga as early as the eighth century A.D.

Tibetan dream yoga is a complex system that pays attention to sleeping postures, uses different times of night for varying types of incubation, and employs a wide range of visualisation and meditative techniques to bring about the induction of lucid dreaming and its control. In some schools of Tibetan dream yoga, still taught today, the students take a vow never to lie down straight to sleep, and have thongs with which to tie their legs into a crouching position when they go to sleep.

During a period when he was following dream yoga practice, anthropologist Charles Laughlin used an open-sided box to sleep in. This was too small to allow him to lie down fully, so, in dream yoga tradition, he prevented himself from stretching out to sleep, and had to sleep for months in a semi-reclining position. Laughlin found that rarely a night passed without him experiencing lucidity in his dreaming.

One Tantric injunction states that to achieve what we would call a lucid dream, one has to place oneself "at the junction between waking and sleeping", or what we now call the hypnogogic (falling asleep) and hypnopompic (awakening from sleep) states. The ultimate aim of dream yoga is to wake up from this dream, the dream of life, as well as from the veils of illusion we find in dreams. The dream yoga master can pass through all mental states without there being any discontinuity in his level of awareness. For him, it is more a case of switching channels in the mind, all of them equally illusory, painted like transparent coloured inks on the clear surface of the Void, the Perfect Mind.

Early Lucid Dreaming in the West

Lucid dreaming in the West seems to have been known about since at least the fourth century B.C. when Aristotle wrote that "often when one is asleep, there is something in consciousness which declares that what then presents itself is but a dream". The first actually documented account, however, seems to have been made by St. Augustine in 415 A.D. when he referred in a letter to two dreams experienced by Gennadius, a Roman physician. According to Augustine, the good doctor had a dream in which he was approached by a youth of marvellous appearance who led him to a city where he heard "exquisitely sweet" singing and music. The youth told Gennadius that it was "the hymn of the blessed and holy". The following night the youth appeared again to the Roman in a dream. The youth asked if Gennadius recognised him, and the man said he certainly did, that he had been his guide in his dream the previous night. The youth acknowledged that they had met while Gennadius had been asleep, and that indeed he was asleep now. He asked where the man thought his body was at that moment, to which Gennadius answered, "In my bed". The fact that many centuries later St. Thomas Aquinas could observe that "while asleep a man may judge that what he sees is a dream" hints that lucid dreaming was a known condition of mind in medieval Christianity.

We have already seen that the Islamic world had a deep respect for dreams, so it is not surprising that a famous twelfth-century Spanish Sufi, Ibn El-Arabi, could write that "a person must control his thoughts in a dream. The training of this alertness ... will produce great benefits for the individual". But the history of lucid dreaming does not take on substance as far as we are concerned until the nineteenth century, and even then it emerged only from the shadows of more mainstream sleep and dream investigation. As we follow this history, we will come to learn the main characteristics of lucid dreaming

Modern Pioneers of Lucidity

The first major pioneer was the Marquis d'Hervey de Saint-Denys, who we met in the previous chapter. He was a scholar of Chinese literature by profession, but a meticulous observer of his dream life in private. Starting early in his teens, he went on to fill twenty-two volumes or albums with self-observations of his dreams, making great use of visual depictions. His dream record covered 1946 nights. In 1867, he published a book, *Les rêves et les moyens de les diriger*, which described these personal explorations. He castigated the scientific community of his day for doing so little about studying the nature of dreaming. He was particularly withering about psychologists and brain researchers who failed to study their own dreams directly.

In the course of his diligent dream studies, Saint-Denys uncovered what Van de Castle has called "the rules of syntax which govern the structure of dreams". He made observations about memory, the association of ideas, sensations and images in dreams and other factors which later researchers would weave into dream theory. He also provided vivid descriptions of the geometric entoptic imagery so often experienced during the hypnogogic phase. But it is his work on lucid dreams that especially interests us here. It was not until he was well into his dream research that Saint-Denys experienced lucidity. This so impressed him that he developed techniques based on pre-sleep autosuggestion to allow him to transfer the "faculties of attention and will" to his dreaming mind. Within six months, he was having lucid dreams "on average two nights out of five, and after a year three nights out of four." Within fifteen months, Saint-Denys was experiencing a lucid dream "almost every night". He stated that "the new consciousness and freedom of mind" acquired by the aware dreamer allowed unpleasant dreams to be controlled in such a way as to eliminate the negative features. "The fear of disagreeable visions weakens as we perceive how foolish it is, and the desire to see agreeable ones becomes more active as we develop a growing power to induce them of our own accord," Saint-Denys observed. This was perhaps the first research statement to indicate that one could not only become conscious in dreams, but could also learn to control their outcome as well.

In one of his lucid dreams, Saint-Denys leapt from the top of a tall building "full of anxious curiosity" as to what would happen. As he fell, the scene suddenly changed, and he was in a crowd clustering around a dead man. As the corpse was being carried away on a stretcher, someone in the crowd told him that the man had thrown himself off the cathedral tower. This fitted in with the Frenchman's belief that he couldn't experience in a dream anything he hadn't already experienced in waking life, as he felt all dreams, lucid and otherwise, essentially involved the recall of memory material, no matter how creatively transfigured it might be. It is difficult to accept Saint-Denys' premise

Saint-Denys deliberately sought out dangerous or frightening situations in his lucid dreams to test his ability to avert a negative outcome. He found by fixing his eyes on pursuing monsters, for example, he could make them slow down and disintegrate into floating clumps of material. Another technique was to cover his dream eyes with his dream hands, allowing him to change a frightening scene into another, happier one.

completely, though, as the lucid dreamer often experiences vivid sensations of flying as free as a bird, which can hardly have been part of normal waking experience.

Saint-Denys coined the term "lucid dream" (*"rêve lucide"*) and proclaimed that lucid dreaming could be learned. It is a particularly sad fact, therefore, that his book was not widely read, and became something of a collector's item. So obscure did it become, in fact, that Freud was unable to locate a copy to study while researching his magnum opus. Consequently, the first edition of *The Interpretation of Dreams* contained no direct reference to lucid dreaming. In the next, 1909, edition, however, he does make a reference, saying that "there are some people who are clearly aware during the night that they are asleep and dreaming and who thus seem to possess the faculty of consciously directing their dreams". It was only in the 1914 edition that Freud mentioned Saint-Denys, and then only from a secondary reference. More than one of today's researchers have openly speculated that the history of dream research – and psychoanalysis – in the twentieth century might have been dramatically different if only Freud had been able to properly study Saint-Denys and fully grasp not only the nature of lucid dreaming but also that it could be learned. As it was, the matter of lucidity in dreaming arose in the nineteenth-century literature only sporadically.

Frederic Myers, the Cambridge professor who coined the term "telepathy" and co-founded the Society for Psychical Research, was naturally intrigued with the idea of lucid dreaming. He wasn't very good at practicing it, though, claiming that despite painstaking effort he achieved lucidity on only three nights out of about three thousand. Nevertheless, he experienced enough to know that the lucid dream was a remarkable and important mental state. In an 1887 account, he described one of his dreams in which he found himself standing in his study. He suddenly realised he was dreaming because he couldn't focus properly on the furniture. On becoming lucid, he experienced that urge felt by many first-time lucid dreamers to meet a person in the dream – a desire generally tinged with a little apprehension. Myers wanted to know if such lucid dream characters "were like the real persons, and how they behaved". So he left his dream study, and cautiously walked down the stairs in the dream house. The stair carpet wasn't the same as in real life, being more threadbare – "apparently generalised from memories of seaside lodgings". He decided to call one of his servants. The pantry door opened but the person who emerged was quite unlike any of his servants in waking life. "This is all I can say," Myers reported ruefully, "for the excitement of perceiving that I had created a new personage woke me with a shock." This is a common reaction with inexperienced lucid dreamers, for it is one thing to gaze upon inanimate objects in a lucid dream, but quite another to confront facsimile life.

French researcher, Yves Delage, published his work on dreams in 1891. Like Saint-Denys, in several of his lucid dreams Delage admitted to having "thrown myself on purpose into some danger in order to see what would come of it". Around the same time, Ernst Mach of the University of Vienna was experiencing lucid dreams. At one time, when he was absorbed in the problem of how we perceive space, he had a dream in which he was walking through a wood. He noticed that the displacement of the trees as he moved was not quite right, and this made him aware that he was dreaming. As the dream turned lucid, the "missing displacements ... were immediately supplied".

What was to be a delayed breakthrough in lucid dream research came in 1913, with the publication of a paper he gave to the Society for Psychical Research by Fredrik Van Eeden, a Dutch psychiatrist and author. He reported that he had been keeping a dream journal since 1896, but from 1898 "began to keep a separate account for a particular kind of dream". He collected over 350 reports of these special dreams in which he had "a full recollection of my day-life, and could act voluntarily, though I was so fast asleep that no bodily sensations penetrated into my perception". Like Saint-Denys, to whom he referred, Van Eeden called these special dreams "lucid dreams", and it is to him rather than Saint-Denys that we owe the use of the term today. He made it quite clear that he was distinguishing lucid dreaming from ordinary and, even, vivid dreaming. Despite the fact that during lucidity one is awake within a dream, Van Eeden noted that "the sleep, as I am able confidently to state, is undisturbed, deep and refreshing".

Van Eeden made a number of important observations about lucid dreaming, of interest to anyone intending to take up the practice today. One concerned what he called the dream-body. "In a lucid dream the sensation of having a body ... is perfectly distinct; yet I know at the same time that the physical body is sleeping and has quite a different position," he wrote. "In waking up the two sensations blend together, so to speak, and I remember as clearly the action of the dream-body as the restfulness of the physical body." He made a special point of mentioning that most of his lucid dreams occurred in the hours between five and eight in the morning, citing Dante who claimed that period to be when "our mind is least clogged by the material body". We of course now know this is generally the time when the longest periods of REM sleep occur in the normal nightly sleep cycle.

It appears that as his experience increased over the years, Van Eeden was able to prolong the duration of his lucid dreams, which seem to have occurred spontaneously, for he does not describe any specific exercises. He was most impressed with the sound of his voice during lucid dreaming. "I use my voice as loudly as I can, and though I know quite well that my physical body is lying in profound sleep, I can hardly believe that this loud voice is inaudible in the waking world. Yet, though I have sung, shouted, and spoken loudly in hundreds of dreams, my wife has never heard my voice. . ."

Like other lucid dream pioneers, Van Eeden was tempted to experiment. In one lucid dream, he failed in an attempt to break a piece of glass, so then he took a claret glass from a table and struck it forcibly with his fist – remarking to himself how dangerous this would be in waking life. That didn't break either. "But lo! when I looked at it again after some time, it

Van Eeden found that recurring flying or floating sensations in ordinary dreams were often an indication that lucid dreams were coming. "And the lucid dream itself is often initiated and accompanied all the time by the sensation of flying," he further observed. "Sometimes I find myself floating swiftly through wide spaces; once I flew backwards, and once, dreaming that I was inside a cathedral, I flew upwards, with the immense building and all in it, at great speed." The newcomer to lucid dreaming soon discovers that the sensation of flying is, indeed, one of the classic hallmarks of the mental state.

was broken. It broke all right, but a little too late, like an actor who misses his cue. This gave me a very curious impression of being in a fake-world, cleverly imitated, but with small failures." Some of his other experiments underlined the fact that all the senses can be involved in lucid dreams. In one lucid dream he marked a cross on the palm of his left dream hand with spittle, and was able to press it against his dream cheek and feel its wetness. Upon awaking, his physical hand was, of course, perfectly dry. In another experiment, Van Eeden saw a decanter of claret in a lucid dream, and so he tasted it. "Well, we can also have voluntary impressions of taste in this dream-world; this has quite the taste of wine," the Dutch researcher said to himself in the dream.

Van Eeden also touched on another experience often loosely associated with lucid dreaming. He rather clumsily referred to it as the "wrong-waking-up-dream", nowadays more usually called the "false awakening". He sometimes found that after a lucid dream he would think he had woken up in his bedroom, until some inconsistency made him realise that he was still dreaming. This effect has been widely reported in the dream literature – sometimes false awakenings occur near the end of a night of normal dreaming. These false awakenings seem to have the clarity and realism of lucid dreams, but the fact that the dreamer thinks they are real shows that the critical faculty is not fully operational, so they cannot be considered as true lucid dreams. We will return to their importance in a later chapter.

Though Van Eeden's paper was not particularly long, it clearly covered a comprehensive range of features associated with lucid dreaming, and underpinned many aspects of modern lucid dream investigation. But that did not happen straight away; lucid dreaming continued to find little favour as the decades of the twentieth century rolled by. In 1921, Mary Arnold-Foster published her *Studies in Dreams*. It appears the Englishwoman was unaware of Saint-Denys' work, and recounts her own individual experiments. She also used pre-sleep autosuggestion to make herself wake up in her dreams, and she went into considerable detail about how she flew during her dreams. "The actual process by which I fly in my dreams has always been the same since the earliest days when I first fluttered down the nursery staircase," she wrote, indicating how long she had been familiar with her dream life. She normally just pushed herself off from the ground with her feet and floated away, but if she wanted a bit more acceleration or extra altitude she would paddle the air with her hands. "If I am at all fatigued by a long flight, this motion of the hands is of great assistance and gives confidence and increased power," she added. Arnold-Foster even had a special "flying dress" she wore in her dreams! By using alarm-clock awakenings she confirmed that dreaming occurred only periodically in the night, and disagreed with Freud's emphasis on the pychopathology of dreams.

Another English researcher of the same period was Hugh Calloway, who wrote under the pseudonym of Oliver Fox. He often experienced what he called "The Dream of Knowledge", by which he meant dreams in which one had the knowledge that one was dreaming. His reports, however, like others, came under the Spiritualist-Theosophical banner of "astral projection", and we will look more closely at such work in the final chapter when we consider the similarities between lucid dreams and the out-of-body experience.

A scatter of people wrote on the topic over the following decades. Russian philosopher P.D. Ouspensky referred

Fig. 7: A characteristic experience in lucid dreaming (and, as we shall see, in the closely related out-of-body and certain mind-altering drug experiences, as well as in the traditional shamanic trance) is the sensation of being able to fly as free as a bird – or even as a bird in some cases.

occasionally to "half-dream states" in which he saw how dreams were created and in which he could exercise control. The Russian offered a new twist in that rather than waking within a dream, he entered his lucid dreams by maintaining his awareness as he passed through the hypnogogic state from waking to sleep. His most usual methods of locomotion in his lucid dreams were flying or scrambling along on all fours.

In 1936, Alward Embury Brown wrote a paper for the *Journal of Abnormal Psychology* on "Dreams in Which the Dreamer Knows He is Asleep". A couple of years later, Harold von Moers-Messmer reported on twenty-two of his lucid dreams in a German psychology journal. A decade after that, the American psychiatrist, Nathan Rapport, wrote positively about lucid dreaming in a paper for the *Psychiatric Quarterly*. All these writings involved anecdotal material and self-reports, however, and it wasn't until 1959 at Germany's Johann Wolfgang Goethe University that an effective technique for inducing lucid dreaming was developed and the first systematic investigations involving several subjects took place. By now, the mainstream, scientific dream and sleep laboratory work was yielding dividends, and both scientific and public interest in dreams was aroused, but lucid dreaming was still the poor cousin.

In 1968, the Oxford "psychophysical researcher", Celia Green, published *Lucid Dreams*. This was a no-frills, fairly scholarly exposition of the topic full of anecdotal reports. It introduced some of the lucid dream pioneers and made some pertinent observations about categories of lucid dreams and their circumstances of induction. Ahead of her time, Green also suggested that it should be possible to train subjects to use physical motor functions to signal when they are lucidly dreaming, so these can be recorded on laboratory polygraph equipment. This was an important book, in that it clearly established lucid dreaming as a distinct subject amenable to experimental research. Nevertheless, the book was not very widely read, and because of the research interests of its author, mainstream scientists who did read it tended to dismiss its subject as relating to parapsychology and therefore outside their sphere of interest.

The next important milestone came the following year, when American psychologist Charles Tart published an anthology of papers called *Altered States of Consciousness*. One section of this book dealt with dreams and dreaming, and Tart himself called for the experimental control of dreams. Even more importantly, he republished Van Eeden's 1913 paper, and so the breakthrough that work represented was finally consummated. It was widely read, and was most influential as far as younger workers in the field of dream studies were concerned. In the following several years, psychiatrist Ann Faraday published popular books on dream consciousness and hailed lucid dreaming as "one of the most exciting frontiers of human experience". She considered that it marked a process of self-integration. She was able to have a psychedelic "high" in one of her lucid dreams simply by wishing she had some LSD. In 1974, psychologist and prolific lucid dreamer, Patricia Garfield, published her popular *Creative Dreaming*, giving important information on methods of dream control.

The best-selling books of the late Carlos Castaneda are cited by American lucid dreaming expert, Stephen LaBerge, as being a significant factor in the raising of public interest in dreamwork and lucid dreaming. Although there has been much debate as to whether Castaneda's books are fact, fiction or "faction", it seems that one of the leading players in the book series, the Native American elder, "don Juan" (whether a real person or a character dreamt up – perhaps literally – by Castaneda), was speaking about a mental state akin to lucid dreaming to Carlos, the narrator. Castaneda italicised it as *dreaming*. In *Journey to Ixtlan*, there is a scene where Carlos is taught to focus on his hands while *dreaming*. As many lucid dreamers have subsequently discovered, looking at the dream-body's hands can have the distinct effect of stabilising a lucid dream that is on the verge of collapsing back into normal, unaware dreaming, or being extinguished by wakefulness.

On the other side of the equation, however, most sleep and dream researchers continued to dismiss the possibility of lucid dreaming. One philosopher of science dismissed all dream recall and research as "irrelevant" and "meaningless", claiming that nothing was experienced during sleep! Those studying neurophysiology considered lucid dreaming as an unlikely phenomenon not worth investigating. Some researchers, such as Ernest Hartmann of Tufts University, accepted that lucid dreams could occasionally occur, but argued that they were not true dreams but rather "brief partial arousals" from sleep. Other orthodox researchers similarly considered lucid dreams to be "momentary physiological awakenings" or "micro-awakenings".

But on the 12th of April, 1975, a quiet experiment at the University of Hull, England, was to prove the sceptics wrong.

SIGNALS FROM THE DREAMWORLD

Psychologist Keith Hearne had been studying aspects of dreams for a few years earlier, before going to Hull to work on his Ph.D. With the arrival of new computer equipment at the psychology department, Hearne busied himself with a range of new experiments and studies. Among these were physiological studies of sleeping subjects. In this period, Hearne happened to meet Alan Worsley, a 37-year-old who mentioned that he frequently had lucid dreams. Worsley agreed to act as a subject in Hearne's laboratory. Hearne recalled Charles Tart's observations that if a signalling system could be established between a dreamer and an experimenter, dreams would no longer be simply subjective phenomena. He also recalled Celia Green's suggestion that dream subjects be trained to send signals to the experimenter. Hearne wanted to work out a way of scientifically proving that lucidity was a true mental state. But how? There had been attempts to get dream laboratory subjects to press micro-switches fixed to the hand to indicate when they were in REM sleep, but these had not been successful, there always being evidence that the subject was momentarily awake when making the signal. Hearne realised that one of the key problems was the "paralysis" that occurs in REM sleep, when most muscle groups were damped down. But then it struck him like a thunderbolt that not all muscles are inactive during REM sleep – the respiratory and eye muscles still operated. Perhaps because it was so obvious, no one had thought of using these muscles for signalling from within a lucid dream. So Hearne arranged with Worsley that when he became aware within a dream he was to make a clear set of smooth eye movements to left and right, quite different to the usual random rolling of the eyes in REM sleep, so that they would show distinctly on the chart recording eye movement – the EOG. (Worsley states that it was actually he who suggested this to Hearne – *personal communication*.)

The first attempt failed. (In fact, Worsley had a lucid dream in the morning, just after Hearne had switched off the polygraph equipment!) But a week later, on the 12th of April, everything worked according to plan. Hearne was wearily studying the chart spewing out of the recording apparatus: it was now a few minutes past eight in the morning and it had been a long and a tiring vigil through the night. Worsley had been dreaming for about half an hour. "Suddenly, out of the jumbled senseless to's and fro's of the two eye-movement recording channels, a regular set of large zig-zags appeared on the chart," Hearne recalled in his book, *The Dream Machine*. "Instantly, I was alert and felt the greatest exhilaration on realising that I was observing the first ever deliberate signals sent from within a dream to the outside. The signals were coming from another world – the world of dreams – and they were as exciting as if they were emanating from some other solar system in space."

Alan Worsley had been dreaming that he was wandering around the university wearing electrodes. The novelty of the situation suddenly made him realise that he was dreaming, and he immediately made the eye signals. While still within a dream and physiologically asleep, as proven by the polygraph recordings, Worsley had been able to become conscious and take deliberate, rational action based on his pre-sleep memory. The reality of lucid dreaming had been demonstrated.

Hearne decided to devote his PhD to lucid dreaming, and moved to Liverpool University to work on it. He was in virgin territory, and the data he began to accumulate was all new and exciting. In his first lucid dream study, still using Alan Worsley as subject, eight complete lucid dreams were recorded on the polygraph. Worsley's lucid dreams lasted from one to six minutes in length, and usually occurred between 6.30 am and 8 am, in the midst of REM sleep. A lucid dream would occur on average twenty-four minutes after the onset of a REM period. An intriguing discovery was that lucidity was invariably preceded by a burst of REM activity. By using coded eye movements during lucid episodes, it was possible to confirm that lucid dreams happened in real time. In other words, events in a lucid dream actually took the time they seemed to take to the lucid dreamer.

Hearne discovered that while in a lucid dream, a subject could also voluntarily alter his breathing rate as well as the eye movements – this provided another means of communication.

A few months after his initial success at Hull, Hearne had informed the renowned sleep and dream researcher Allan Rechtschaffen at Chicago University, who had responded by encouraging the young researcher in his efforts. In 1977, Hearne delivered a paper to a conference on Behavioural Sciences, but the scientific establishment resisted accepting his results. A version of the paper was submitted to the prestigious British science journal, *Nature*, but it was rejected by the editor on the grounds that "it would not command wide enough an audience in the scientific community". A paper was also rejected by the journal, *Psychophysiology*. A technical article appeared in the *Nursing Mirror* in 1980, but other papers by Hearne appeared only in the *Journal of the Society for Psychical Research*, an excellent publication but one which gave the material a "fringe" context causing most mainstream scientists to miss it or dismiss it. Hearne's PhD thesis was published by the University of Liverpool in 1978.

Two years after Hearne's initial breakthrough, Stephen LaBerge in California was also on the trail of lucid dreams. He already knew of Van Eeden and Tibetan dream yoga, but then he came across Celia Green's book. Just reading about lucid dreaming caused him to have several lucid dreams of his own (a phenomenon that the reader of this book might well experience). He realised it was a learnable ability, and within seven years LaBerge had accumulated almost nine hundred personal lucid dream reports. LaBerge, too, had been alerted by Charles Tart's writings to the possibility of communicating to the outside world from within a lucid dream. LaBerge, independently of Hearne, figured that eye movements offered a way of accomplishing the signalling procedure. In his own lucid dreams, he had discovered that he could move his dream eyes at will, and guessed that these would be movements of his physical eyes also. He needed a dream laboratory to prove the point, and he was allowed to work on his Ph.D. at the Stanford University Sleep Research Center. Working with Lynn Nagel, LaBerge was able to produce EOG signals from within a lucid dream on 13 January, 1978 – almost three years after Hearne's similar experiment. It was not until September 1979 that the experiment was successfully repeated, however, and LaBerge had a polygraph moved to his home, where he was having more lucid dreams than in the laboratory. By Christmas that year he had another dozen polygraph records of lucid dreams. LaBerge found, as had Hearne, that all his lucid dreams occurred within REM sleep. By 1980, LaBerge was surrounded by a small group of volunteers. They called themselves "oneironauts", based on Greek words meaning dream explorers or adventurers.

The attempt to publish initially proved as frustrating for LaBerge as it had done for Hearne. The major American scientific journal, *Science*, refused a paper. One of the anonymous referees to whom the editor turned for advice couldn't believe that one could signal while having a dream, and cited a 1978 paper by Rechtstaffen on non-reflectiveness in dreams. This was particularly ironic, in that Hearne had sent Rechstaffen the news of his success in recording lucid dream signals a few years earlier. A revised paper was sent to *Science* later, but that too was rejected: it seemed the orthodox experts just couldn't accept that lucid dreaming was possible, or, at least, of any interest. *Nature* refused a paper from LaBerge and Nagel on precisely the same grounds that it had rejected the one from Hearne. In the end, their paper found a home in *Perceptual and Motor Skills*, a valuable but relatively minor scientific publication. LaBerge emphasises that it was therefore still the case, as late as 1980, that most dream researchers rejected lucid dreams as genuine phenomena, viewing them, at best, as "brief daydream-like intrusions of wakefulness into disturbed sleep". But by 1981, LaBerge and colleagues had amassed so much scientific data supporting lucid dreaming that he was able to convince an important scientific conference of their validity, and lucid dreaming finally was granted scientific acceptance. Other labs began to explore the mental state.

Hearne's own difficulties in getting published, allied with his natural caution in trying to avoid formal announcement of his pioneering experiments from being pre-empted, had delayed the news of his work reaching the ears of the American lucid dream workers, and it was not until the autumn of 1980 that LaBerge learned of the earlier successes in Hull and Liverpool. LaBerge admitted to being "astonished". In his 1985 book, *Lucid Dreaming*, LaBerge blames what he calls, perhaps a little unfairly, Hearne's "reticence" and implied secrecy to excuse why his own extensive review of the lucid dream literature in his PhD thesis had failed to pick up "so much as a rumor" of the Englishman's work. Nevertheless, it is primarily to LaBerge that we owe today's burgeoning interest in lucid dreaming. He went on to write best-selling books on the subject and formed the Lucidity Institute, which sells gadgets and literature that aid in the induction of lucid dreaming.

SOME BENEFITS OF LUCID DREAMING

So lucid dreaming is a scientific fact, and it can be an experiential fact for anyone who chooses to learn how to achieve it. It is still a relatively young subject area as far as our culture is concerned, and there is much yet to learn about it both in terms of the nature of the state itself and also how it can be used. Scientific experts and amateur "oneironauts" alike have much to offer the subject, and much to gain from it. We can take a moment here to note just some of the benefits to be had from lucid dreaming.

Adventure

First and foremost is the fun. It does not take much imagination to appreciate how the ultimate form of virtual reality that lucid dreaming represents could present the opportunity to have the experience of visiting distance places on this earth, feasting on staggering vistas, journeying to other worlds, travelling into the past, taking part in thrilling adventures, and so on. But many budding lucid dreamers often have difficulty believing that there could be such a thing as realistic sex in this mental realm. The secret to overcoming this misconception is to realise that all the physical senses have their lucid dreaming equivalents.

Lucid Dream Sex

One of Hearne's informants described a lucid dream in which he was walking round the grounds of his old school when he encountered a tennis teacher as he passed the courts. She ran up to the dreamer, kissed him and pulled him down on top of her. "I took down her pants, and she unzipped me," the man recalled. "She opened her legs and we made love. I even orgasmed with her, in full, and felt an ejaculation inside her.

At this point I awoke." The man did not experience a "wet" dream (in other words, there had been no physical, seminal emission) – causing Hearne to comment in *The Dream Machine* on "the highly cerebral nature of sex in humans". The lucid dreamer felt sad, however, realising that he could never know who the dream woman was nor see her again. Another of Hearne's lucid dreamers found herself making love with the rock star, Sting. "I could actually... feel the softness of the skin – also, the actual sexual act," she reported. Another woman experienced a passionate sexual affair with her brother-in-law in a lucid dream. She marvelled how "everything was so real... I could even smell his after-shave".

Psychotherapist Kenneth Kelzer describes many of his lucid dreams in his book, *The Sun and the Shadow*. In one he is walking through a forest when he encounters a group of Vietnamese women soldiers, dressed in olive-green uniforms. He is attracted to one in particular, and he felt her "powerful sensual-sexual magnetism" drawing him to her. "Eagerly and lovingly, I caress her genitals and I kiss her repeatedly on her face ... [which] has a soft luminous quality as if bathed in moonlight. . ." he writes. One of LaBerge's reports in *Exploring the World of Lucid Dreaming* is the account of a woman who found herself in a lucid dream walking alongside the actor Michael York. They were in a field full of fragrant flowers, and both fell among them, making love. She could feel the softness of the flowers as well as smell their distinctive scent, and was aware of a cool breeze blowing over her and her dream lover as they lay entwined. (The sensation of a cool wind can often figure in lucid dreams.) It is therefore clear that the full range of sensual experience is available in lucid dreams.

Patricia Garfield considers orgasm to be a natural part of lucid dreaming. She claims that two-thirds of her lucid dreams contain sexual elements, and about fifty percent of them result in orgasms. She often found these to be better than in waking life. We know that the genitals are usually aroused during REM sleep and this must play a part in the sensations that can be achieved. In fact, LaBerge and colleagues conducted research to see if there were physiological correlates to sexual experiences in lucid dreams. Their first subject was a woman, since women report more dream orgasms than men do. The subject was asked to make eye movements when she commenced sexual activity in a lucid dream and again when she experienced orgasm. She did as requested, and LaBerge found significant correspondences in the physiological record during the fifteen seconds when the woman was signalling lucid dream orgasm: her vaginal muscle activity, vaginal pulse amplitude and respiration rate reached their highest values of the night. Interestingly, though, her heart rate showed only a slight increase. LaBerge then went on to study two men. Again, respiration rate increased, but there was no significant effect on heart rate. Though both subjects reported realistic ejaculations in their lucid dreams, neither of them had physical emissions.

Lucid dream sex is obviously a boon to anyone who can't get enough of a good thing, but it is of special benefit to people who have disabilities or circumstances that prevent them having a physical sex life. It can also allow experienced lucid dreamers who have such inclinations to explore illicit sexual liaisons, or to experiment with different kinds of sexual activity. And it is all safe sex!

Inspiration and Problem Solving

Any kind of dreaming can result in the unexpected answer to a problem engaging one's waking mind. In lucid dreaming, this can be refined to great accuracy with full conscious recall. "The unconscious is a vast storehouse of knowledge, sensitivity and insight," reminds Kenneth Kelzer. Keith Hearne likewise describes it as "that great treasure-house of originality", and refers to the classic case of Friedrich Kekule, who comprehended the ring-like structure of the benzene molecule through a lucid dream episode that occurred in a hypnogogic state while dozing before the fire. He first saw atoms "gambolling" before his inner vision. "My mental eye, rendered more acute by visions of this kind, could now distinguish larger structures... long rows, sometimes more closely fitted together, all twining and twisting in snakelike motion," Kekule recalled. "But look! What was that? One of the snakes had seized hold of its own tail, and the form whirled mockingly before my eyes." A lucid dream had helped the chemist make a major discovery in organic chemistry.

Problem solving in lucid dreams need not necessarily involve such major scientific discoveries, but it can be just as important to the individual. LaBerge and Rheingold refer to several cases in their *Exploring the World of Lucid Dreaming*. In waking life, one informant had been given an assignment paper containing five problems for a math exam, and mulled them over all day. That night, the person dreamed lucidly of leafing through a particular math reference book. Nothing specific was learned in the dream, but the next day the informant checked that particular book and found it did supply the information necessary to solve one of the problems. This could, perhaps, be seen as extraordinary enhancement of memory within a lucid dream: we all have more knowledge than surfaces in our conscious awareness. In another instance, the same math student was having problems understanding vector spaces, but in a lucid dream was able to perceive directly a four-dimensional space, allowing hugely increased comprehension of the math involved. Such is the model-building capacity of the lucid dreaming mind. Artist Fariba Bogzaran found she became lucid whenever she entered an art gallery in her dreams, and now uses this to discover the subject of her forthcoming works. Hearne similarly claims to have seen numerous original works of art in his lucid dreams, but he points out that those paintings will never see the light of day because he lacks the technical ability to reproduce them. "The dream may provide some marvellous ideas for art, but the practical skills have to exist to externalise images," he warns. Access to such lucid inspiration is only an aid to hard-won mastery of one's chosen form of expression or creativity – be it painting, music, writing, or whatever – not a substitute for it.

While both ordinary dreams and lucid dreams can occasionally provide spontaneous help with problems, it is more usual that the lucid dream has to be controlled in order to access the information being sought. "In such a way, a composer, say, might decide in the dream to enter a concert hall and hear a new piece, or a poet might enter a library and look at a poem never before seen, or an architect might gaze upon some spectacular new building," Hearne advises.

Lucid Dreaming as Rehearsal

Because of the exceptional realism of lucid dreams, it is possible for experienced lucid dreamers to test out situations, such as rehearsing conversations with people who are to be met shortly in waking life, trying out interview strategies, and practicing specific skills, in much the same way that pilots, drivers, astronauts, military personnel and others can practice tasks in computerised virtual reality exercises, only more so. Paul Tholey, who was a leading German lucid dream researcher, remarked on the realism of the dream-body's movements in lucid dreams. One of the present authors (P.D.) can confirm this. He found himself flying high in one particularly strong lucid dream, and could not resist arching backwards through the air, looping-the-loop in the great blue vault of the sky. The sensation was totally realistic: he could feel the air brushing over his body and the muscles tightening and relaxing appropriately as he manoeuvred. If he could really fly, he knew, this is exactly what it would feel like. Because such convincing bodily sensations occur in lucid dreaming, Tholey found he was able to practice specific skiing exercises in his lucid dreams that he maintained definitely helped him improve his actual, physical skiing ability. His balance and bodily tensions could be honed on the ski slopes of the mind. Similarly, one of LaBerge's informants told how she was so able to improve her tennis performance in lucid dreaming that she credited it with helping her win a tournament, an accomplishment that astonished her teacher and friends. Another case involved an ice hockey player who improved her game by "surrendering to the quality of complete skating" in a lucid dream. In the safety of the lucid dream situation, she was able to learn to overcome residual fear and hold nothing back, so her skating became fluid and free – she learned how to enter this "surrender" state of mind during her physical skating. In another line of activity altogether, a computer programmer found that she was able to "run" and correct programs she had written in waking life in her lucid dreams before she ever sat down before a physical keyboard to test them. It saved her untold hours of real time. Lucid dream rehearsal can even extend to sex! In one of Hearne's cases, a 17-year-old virgin admitted "I experiment sexually in my lucid dreams".

Whether in sport, business, or personal life, the ability to conduct lucid dream rehearsals can be a fantastic advantage to have. Lucid dreaming can have a great effect on waking life in all sorts of ways, but, as ever, it relies on the dreamer having the skills and disciplines to make use of the lucid dreaming advantage.

Paranormal Research

The gift lucid dreaming gives the individual in observing how dreams are constructed, and how the mind operates, has already been hinted at in earlier pages. There is no doubt that lucid dreaming will open up whole new chapters in consciousness research. Much of this will seem highly specialised and beyond the interests of everyday life. One area where it may impact more noticeably for most people, however, is in the realm of paranormal research. We have already learned that some research, notably at Maimonides, has indicated that ESP abilities are heightened in dreaming states. Although the mainstream view is that paranormal events do not happen, practicing lucid dreamers can arrive at their own conclusions by making their own tests.

Some paranormal hints already exist in the lucid dream literature, primarily relating to precognitive (prophetic) lucid dreams, and the question of whether the lucid dreamer's mind can visit distant places. Van Eeden, the lucid dream pioneer, reported a precognitive experience in a lucid dream. In the dream, he found himself in a small Dutch town where he met his brother-in-law, who Van Eeden, being lucid, knew was dead. The deceased man warned Van Eeden that he was heading for a financial crisis, in which he would be robbed of 10,000 guilders. Van Eeden awoke puzzled: there was not the slightest hint of any impending disaster, and he was not even in possession of the money referred to. Yet the dream occurred just when there were railways strikes in Holland, and it was this, Van Eeden realised in retrospect, that eventually led up to the events that were, indeed, to cost him dear. In fact, Van Eeden lost more than the foretold amount.

Hugh Calloway ("Oliver Fox") reported a number of apparently paranormal lucid dreams, or "dreams of knowledge" as he called them. One occurred on the eve of his sitting an examination in machine construction. In it, he saw the examination paper, and memorised two of the questions on it. When he came to sit the actual exam the next day, the two items he had memorised duly appeared as sections of larger questions. In another instance, Calloway experienced a false awakening in which he saw the apparition of his girlfriend, Elsie. On meeting her later, she claimed she had visited his room during "travelling clairvoyance", and proceeded to describe minute details in it, even though she had never been there physically. Ironically, Elsie had performed this demonstration to warn Calloway to stop his experiments.

Celia Green quotes a case in which a lucid dreamer decided to visit his son. The impression of contact was made, but the dreamer felt that he could not stay long because he felt "muzzy". When the two met next day for lunch, the first thing the son did was to repeat those words, saying he had had a dream in which he was being visited by the parent.

One of Hearne's cases involved a lucid dreamer who visited a friend in a dream and later described to the friend what he had been seen to be doing, and approximately at what time. The friend was surprised, confirming that he actually had been doing what was described at the appropriate time. Keith Hearne also recalls that in his first lucid dream he met a girl he had never seen before on a beach. She told him that her name was Jane. About three weeks later he met a young woman who was identical in appearance to his dream girl. And yes, it transpired that her name was Jane.

In order to test for paranormal effects, the lucid dreamer generally needs to work out a strategy. When wanting to meet a person, living or dead, in his lucid dreams, Van Eeden would "call" or summon them to see if they would appear. One could also try to modify the plot of a lucid dream so that the desired person would appear naturally as part of the story line. Hearne also suggests the simple expediency of a telephone call in a lucid dream! Some scenario is often required, at any rate, in which communication with a specific (living) person can take place. The lucid dreamer can then check later with the person in question to see if they were aware of any contact occurring. Talking with a dead person in a lucid dream could enable the lucid dreamer to come to his own ideas about whether or not there is survival after death, and it can also have a healing dimension (see below). For precognition, we might try to arrange to see a future edition of a newspaper in a dream, devise a lucid dream time machine, or some other ruse. As for viewing things at a distance, this brings us to deep questions about the out-of-body experience, which we will consider in the final chapter.

Healing and Personal Development

We can see the potential lucid dreaming has for the handling of grief. Many of us will have had the gut-wrenching experience of losing a close relative or dear friend and of being painfully aware that things were left unsaid, issues left unresolved. In the lucid dream one has the potential of meeting that person, seeing them just as they appeared in life, and interacting with them once again. It doesn't matter whether one believes the figure to be a truly discarnate spirit, or a memory-model restored to life by the fabulous wizardry of the mind-brain in lucid dreaming mode, the emotional healing potential of working through unfinished business, even of simply saying "Sorry" or "I love you" and hugging the person, cannot be overstated.

Clearly, such "psychodrama" therapy could be extended to many other inter-personal problems and difficulties with self-image, sense of self-worth, and so on. It can also help you make decisions about the way you are living your life. Used with proficiency and skill, lucid dreaming can make you a happier and psychologically healthier person – indeed, numerous lucid dreamers have remarked how uplifted and well they feel after having had a lucid dream.

Lucid dreaming might also be able to help in physical healing. The use of visualisation in cancer therapy is considered by some experts to be highly effective. Patients visualising tumours or cancerous cells being zapped by white light or even being eaten away by the computer-game Pac-man figure have all reportedly had positive results. Experimental results also indicate that creative visualisation can positively affect a person's immune system. But even powerful visualisation in the waking state is a weak sham compared to the vivid, total

People haunted by nightmares can learn to become lucid in them and so consciously face the hostile or threatening situation, thereby developing their inner strength by observing how fears can be overcome. Lucid dreams can also become psychodramas, where psychological problems are played out – characters (aspects of the self) in a lucid dream can be openly, consciously questioned, and the dreamer's psychological problems and dynamics unravelled. Lucid dreams can be a royal road to mental wholeness.

realism of lucid dream imagery. And we have already seen that sexual imagery in lucid dreaming does involve physiological interaction, so there may well be a true mind-body link that lucid dreaming can help to exploit. Meditation is the means usually employed for healing visualisation techniques, and scientific tests have shown very clearly that meditation can reduce stress, and therefore the illnesses that can derive from it. Some of those studying meditation now think that it can merge into a form of lucid dreaming.

There is a great deal to learn in this little-understood area of healing, and lucid dreaming may well prove to be a key tool in this process. Lucid dreaming represents an exceptional resource for powerful creative visualisation.

Mystical or Peak Experience

Lucid dreaming is remarkable in that it can also allow experimentation in mystical experience. "The lucid dream provides ... a 'psycho-spiritual laboratory'", Kenneth Kelzer accurately observes. In this regard, lucid dreaming becomes a form of spiritual exercise. The nature of the peak experience is essentially that of transcendentalism, the freeing of one's soul or mind from time and space, of the mundane ego, and moving towards the ultimate wholeness, of becoming one with the Divine Ground, the godhead, the void, or whatever other term we choose, depending on our cultural and religious background. Stephen LaBerge has reported one of his own lucid dream mystical experiences. He was driving along a road in his sports car through vibrant scenery, conscious that he was dreaming. He passed an attractive young hitchhiker but coyly remarked "I've had that dream before" and decided to seek something new. He resolved to reach "the Highest". Straight away, his car took off like a rocket into the clouds where he saw a cross on a steeple, a Star of David, and other religious symbols. As he rose even higher, he seemed to enter "a vast mystical realm: a vast emptiness that was yet full of love". He began to sing "with ecstatic inspiration" so that his voice seemed to fill the entire cosmos.

British psychologist Sue Blackmore had a profound and long lucid dream, near the end of which she tried to expand the size of her dream-body, but overshot in her effort and soon found herself encompassing the building she was in, the ground and the sky above, then the whole planet, the solar system and "finally what I took to be the Universe". What followed, she said, she would describe as a religious experience, and felt that her little struggles were being kindly and laughingly watched.

"Transcendental experiences are advantageous, in my view," LaBerge writes in *Lucid Dreaming*, "in that they help us detach from fixed ideas about ourselves. The less we identify with who we think we are (the ego), the more likely it is that we may one day discover who we really are." He points out that lucid dreaming is useful to this end because in a lucid dream the ego, the dream-self, is not having the dream, but *is itself being dreamed*: we can begin to study the ego as a mere projection, which it is likewise in waking, "real" life. It becomes easier to separate ego from true self. LaBerge remarks that following the whims of the ego as one can in lucid dreams eventually becomes a barren exercise – lucid dreamers grow weary of "being the same self night after night...at this point the need for self-transcendence may arise". LaBerge recommends developing lucid dream strategies in order to transcend everyday levels of consciousness.

Fig. 8: Seeking enlightenment: experienced lucid dreamers can aspire to mystical experiences, to "going beyond" mundane time and space.

For those with more modest spiritual aspirations, lucid dreams are the ideal forum in which to meet and discuss the meaning of life with favourite religious figures or the philosophers of antiquity. These dream figures will allow you to communicate directly with the ageless, cellular wisdom held within the hidden dimensions of your mind.

We have learned about the basic history of lucid dreaming, its main characteristics and the typical kinds of experience it can offer; it is time now to study the practical aspects related to accessing this greatest of all forms of virtual reality.

CHAPTER 3

THROUGH THE GATE OF DREAMS

UNLESS you bring your sleeping, dreaming life into focus, you cannot expect to succeed in developing a successful, ongoing lucid dreaming future. Normal dreaming provides the most usual and reliable access to the realms of dreaming lucidity, and so that is where to begin practical work.

Most of us recall occasional vivid dreams and nightmares in a patchy fashion but it is necessary to become much more conscious and coherent about your dream life than that. Some people even claim they don't dream at all! What they mean is, they don't think they dream because they don't remember any. None of this is satisfactory for the aspiring lucid dreamer, and committed effort allied with helpful aids and techniques is required to remedy the situation. Vivid, robust dreams and a good dream recall provide the foundations for lucid dreaming. Everything that is needed to achieve this can be found in this chapter. Serious dreamwork breaks down into these basic areas:

- Strengthening your dreaming ability.
- Learning to remember your dreams, and recording them.
- Trying to understand over time how your dreams seem to be speaking you.
- How to use one's dreams for specific purposes: incubation.

Let us explore these areas, starting with the key factor as far as the quest for dream lucidity is concerned – the ability to have strong dreams.

SUPERCHARGING YOUR DREAMING

If your dream life is rather weak, with poor, extremely fragmented and vague dream recall, or none at all, then the first thing to do is to give your on-board dream machine a boost. Decide on one or two nights each week to concentrate on your dreams, letting the other nights just be your normal schedule. Make an issue of the chosen nights: mark them well ahead on your wall calendar or in your diary, so you have a background awareness of your upcoming dates with dreaming. This will alert and prime your subconscious mind. It is probably best if you keep your selected nights to the same ones each week, but this is not essential – be as flexible as circumstance demand. When these selected "dream awareness" nights come round, you can try one or more of the following techniques and aids, one at a time or in suitable combinations.

A Place to Dream

It was noted in Chapter 1 that the ancient Greeks had special dream temples, with cells called *abatons* in which to have the desired dream. You can create something similar, if a little less ambitious. If you have a spare bed in your home, then use that on your special dreaming nights. Or if you have a comfortable sofa, make that your "abaton". If neither of these options are open to you, then do something different to your bedroom on the appropriate nights (and only on those nights), such as laying a special bedspread on the bed, putting up a picture or poster of a dream-like scene on your bedroom wall, or whatever you choose. This specific alteration of your sleep setting will have a significant effect on your dreaming mind just by itself – it has been found in experiments, for example, that the environment of a dream laboratory has a distinct effect on the dreams of subjects. It is a way of signalling your conscious intent to your subconscious mind.

Eat Your Way to Dreamland

Certain foods tend to promote strong dreams, the infamous example, of course, being cheese. Better, however, is a dish, such as spinach pie, that uses nutmeg, eaten just a few hours before retiring to bed. Comb through your cookery books for recipes for this or other dishes that require, or can require, spicing with nutmeg, and when preparing the food, add a particularly generous pinch of the spice (though not enough to ruin the meal, of course). Nutmeg is metabolised in the body to create a hallucinogen that can greatly assist the brain's own mind-altering neurotransmitters in the production of robust dreams. Another dietary dream-enhancing option is vitamin B6. This significantly increases both the intensity and frequency of dreams. You can take this as a dietary supplement (remember never to exceed the dosage indicated on the bottle), as well as making sure to eat foods rich in B6 such as avocados, brewer's yeast, raw wheat germ, molasses, meat, soya beans, broad beans, bananas, pears, whole grains, salmon, herring, cabbage, green vegetables, eggs.

egg custard

As well as food and drinks that can aid dreaming, it is worth being aware that there are some that can inhibit it. Alcohol, as a prime example, reduces REM sleep.

Pillow Talk

Another way of giving yourself a literal head start in the dream stakes is by making your pillow your ally. Stuff it with several ounces of dry mugwort (*Artemisia vulgaris*), obtainable from any herbal supplier or even some health food shops. Mugwort can promote vigorous dreaming, and American herbalist, Jeannie Rose, specifically recommends it for that purpose – she has described some of her own dramatic dreams had with the use of the herb. Putting out this pillow on those nights when you want to focus on dreaming could become part of your bedtime ritual. It is in any case advised that you do not use this pillow every night. IMPORTANT NOTE: Mugwort contains thujone, which is an abortifacient, so pregnant women should not use this herb.

On the Scent of Dreams

Another olfactory aid to dreaming can be Clary Sage (*Salvia sclarea*) essential oil. It is a hypnotic oil, and in most people it will cause pleasant relaxation (it can be used to treat asthma for this reason). In many people, it will promote dreams as well, and a few may find it produces a sense of euphoria. Sprinkle a few drops of the neat oil directly on your pillow, or, *if it is in a base such as grapeseed oil*, apply it to those areas of your body where it will be quickly and effectively absorbed, such as the "third eye" position in the centre of the forehead, the temples, or the armpits. Apply just a smear of the oil to one or more of these locations. Again, this could become part of your bedtime dreaming ritual, quite apart from the psychoactive properties of the oil. IMPORTANT NOTE: to obtain the best effect from the Clary Sage, ensure that you eat fairly lightly throughout the day, and *don't* mix its use with "dream eating" or the mugwort pillow described above. Also, be careful not to use Clary Sage in conjunction with alcohol, as this is likely to generate powerful nightmares.

The Menstrual Cycle

Women might find that they have better dream recall at certain times in their menstrual cycle than at others. In *Creative Dreaming*, Patricia Garfield reports that she kept a record of her cycle, and found that there was a high peak of dream recall around the middle of it (days 6-19). Dream recall was lower during menses, the first five days of the menstrual cycle, counting the first day of bleeding as day 1. Another low period was between days 20-27.

Bedtime Rituals

Make the process of going to sleep with dreaming in mind as deliberate and conscious as possible. There are a number of ways of doing this, but they essentially boil down to conducting personal rituals at bedtime. Undertake the type of deliberate actions that not only will focus the conscious mind, but that will speak easily to the subconscious mind, which has been the purpose of ritual through the ages. Perhaps light incense (in a safe holder) that you use only in association with your dreamwork (another way of altering your sleeping environment), then stand at the foot of the bed openly intoning or mentally reciting a short intention to dream vividly tonight. This could be elaborated into your own special "Prayer to Morpheus", the ancient Greek god of dreams. Make it an invocation. It could run something like:

> I appeal to you, Morpheus, Lord of Dreams, to grant me visions this night; turn my pillow into a pillar of dreams, and cause my soul to take flight!

And so on: it can be any set of actions you wish – even standing on your head if that helps! It is just a question of making going to bed to dream a noteworthy and purposeful act, rather than just "crashing out" tired without any specific intentions.

All these procedures are part of *incubating* dreams: it helps to take the "perchance" away from "to dream".

KEEPING A DREAM JOURNAL

The only truly effective way to systematically observe your dreams is to maintain a dream journal. The very act of doing this will also enhance your dream recall, in that it helps to programme the unconscious mind. Buy two notebooks, one thicker than the other, each kept specially for recording your dreams, and each distinctive or attractive in some special way. Buy two pens of different colours that you intend to use only for writing down your dreams. If you intend to use illustrations as well as writing to record your dreams (a good idea), then assemble a set of lead and coloured pencils neatly in a sachet for that purpose. Keep one of the pens and thinner notebook conveniently to hand by your bedside. Make a home for the other book, which is to be your dream journal proper, and the other pen and pencils in a special but accessible place – the drawer of a bedside cabinet would make sense.

When you go to bed, spend a few minutes with both notebooks. Take out the thicker notebook, your actual dream journal, and put in the date at the top of a fresh page. In a few lines, summarise your day: very briefly state what you did, how you felt, the weather, anything that specially affected you, and so on. End by writing in when you went to bed. Put the journal away, but leave the thinner, rough notebook open at a fresh page, at the top of which you also write the date, and with the pen lying on it or beside it. Be deliberate and conscious in all these preparations – therefore making them ritualistic. In fact, make the bedside diary or journal a part of your overall dream preparations and programming, especially on your dream-awareness nights. Go to sleep, with the total confidence and expectation that you will remember your dreams in the morning.

Be Still

When you awake in the morning, or if you find yourself waking up in the night, do not move a muscle or open your eyes for a minute or two. When you move and open your eyes, your brain rhythms will start changing, aspects of your brain's chemistry will alter, sensory information will flood into your awareness, and your dream memory will evaporate. Only exceptionally tough dream nuggets are likely to survive, if anything does at all. No wonder that experts reckon up to half the population only remembers about one dream a month! So, before doing anything, lie still, and think of your dreams. If you can't remember anything at all, don't force it – there will be other opportunities. But often you might find yourself recalling just a single element from a dream. As you calmly think about that, other parts of the dream are likely to come to mind, perhaps in a haphazard fashion. Patricia Garfield advises that having completed this process in one bodily position, change to other ones, still with eyes closed, as this may help additional dream recall. When you have the main elements of at least one dream firmly recalled, then you can open your eyes, rise and write them down in very brief note form in your bedside rough notebook. Don't try to order or "smooth" the memories, just jot down everything you can recall, in any order and even if just fragments, and leave it at that for the time being. If you can describe the mood, the emotional afterglow of the dream, put that down too. Then either get up and get on with your day, or go back to sleep, depending on what the situation is.

Later in the day, and certainly before your next dream-awareness night, write up your dream in as coherent a form as possible in your thicker, tidier dream journal. It is considered best to write dream accounts in the present tense.

As you do this, you may possibly recall more about the dream, but be exceptionally careful not to "fill in" any gaps in the dream narrative with invented linking text, or add extraneous thoughts to simplify or "explain" aspects of the dream. If it seems episodic or bizarre, then let it be; just write down as faithful a version as you can. Give the dream in both books the same number: if this is done, you can easily cross-reference the two versions, and also cross-reference between different dreams more readily. Dream psychologist Gayle Delaney usefully recommends marking the various elements of a dream – the dream's setting, the characters, whether human or not, the main objects, feelings, actions – in distinctive ways, such as circling them, putting boxes around the appropriate words, and suchlike, for speedier analysis later on. In this more finished account of your dream, you could add a drawing, a simple sketch or other visual addition to the text. Also, give each dream in your thicker notebook a title. This should summarise the content or main thrust of the dream in a word or a simple phrase. Again, this enables easy reference later (appreciate that you could be looking back over months or even years of your dream records, filling numerous dream journals). Leave the rest of the page or the facing page blank, so you will have room for interpretative notes later on.

If you so wish, you could be very dedicated and on your dream-awareness nights set your alarm at 90-minute intervals through the night, in the hope of being able to remember dreams in your REM periods, and jotting them down. There is no doubt that you are likely to recall more dreams this way, and it is perhaps a good idea for those starting out who are fairly convinced that they do not dream. But it is not a tactic to be maintained for any length of time. One or two nights at the beginning is enough: do not become obsessive about collecting dreams. The plan is simply to improve your ability to recall your dream life, to literally become more conscious of it, and to strengthen your dreaming process. You do not want too many dreams to record, or you might become swamped with them! Take it easy and steady, and trust that you will remember the dreams that you need to.

Try to keep your rough dream notebook by the side of your bed every night, whether or not it is a dream-awareness night, and get into the habit of trying to recall your dreams on as many morning awakenings as you can. Obviously, date and number any dreams recorded in this way too.

INTERPRETING YOUR DREAMS

After some weeks of keeping a dream journal, your dream recall will be improving, and that is the main function of the journal as far as practical lucid dreaming is concerned. Nevertheless, it would be helpful to gain some familiarity with your dreams, including interpreting them, even if that is not your main interest (though most people are fascinated by their dreams!). Even lucid dreams can retain a symbolic and metaphorical character, and when you are literally involved in the imagery of a lucid dream it is important to be aware of this and to recognise it. Tread carefully in dream interpretation, though, for you are entering a minefield. There are many views and schools of thought concerning the nature of dream imagery, and you will need to pick and choose between them, preferably along the lines of advice we give here.

A Multitude of Meanings

In Chapter 1, we saw that Freud essentially considered adult psychopathology to result from childhood fantasies and traumas that had been repressed, and that these stimulated unconscious forbidden desires. He considered that dreams guarded the conscious mind from such repressed subconscious material by allowing their safe expression in sleep. By listening to a patient's dreams and using association techniques, Freud felt he could uncover the root of a neurosis. This is the psychoanalytic approach to dreams, and there are many versions of this, and few therapists now adhere unquestioningly to Freud's more extreme beliefs. As we have seen, the idea of pathologising dreams is particularly unfortunate. Dreams are natural and healthy – and can be of great use to normal, psychologically-healthy individuals as well as those needing psychological healing (though it could be argued that we all need this to some extent). Freud felt that the "latent", repressed material was disguised as symbols fashioned from memories of waking life to make the "manifest" material of the dream palatable. So most key dream images, according to Freud, are really masks for primal repressed material, usually of a sexual nature. So tall, tubular, and "all elongated" objects stood for the phallus, the male organ, while boxes, cases and other hollow vessels of any kind were vulvic symbols. Dreams involving the climbing of ladders, staircases and similar situations represented the sex act. Jung, on the other hand, felt that symbols were deeper psychic creations than this, and could have multiple meanings, To him, a symbol that might represent the male organ to Freud, could have greater meanings of creativity, spiritual insight, and so forth. Sexual dream symbols could represent the mystical wedding of the male and female parts of the self, leading to greater psychic wholeness. He argued that universal symbols could appear in dreams that related to deep-seated, psychic sources he called archetypes, transcending the personal psychology of the dreamer and capable of being found in the world's mythological texts.

Other researchers have come up with multifarious ideas about dream content. The American psychiatrist, Frederic

"Fritz" Perls, founder of Gestalt therapy, proposed that every character and object in a dream represents some facet of the dreamer. He accepted the symbolic nature of dreams, but felt that a dream "is a message of yourself to yourself" containing aspects of the self that have been disowned or projected onto others. Calvin Hall felt that dream images were the visualisations of deep thought processes, and that analysis of a person's dreams could reveal the way the dreamer truly conceptualised the world. Medard Boss treats the dream as a mirror, not looking for deeper meanings behind the imagery, but treating the imagery itself as a metaphorical report of the dreamer's life at that point. And, of course, we must not exclude those who think dreaming is simply the psychic equivalent of garbage disposal, full of the impressions of the day and of no consequence. In this view not only have dreams no value for recalling, they actually should not be remembered. And a close relation to this view is that dreaming is nothing more than an ordering, editing and filtering process about the events and impressions of the day.

Such a diversity of views is exceedingly daunting for the person who hopes to make some sense of the material produced by their dreaming minds. But, in practice, dream interpretation is an accessible goal. In the view of leading dream psychologist, Montague Ullman, the dreamer needs to disengage from "deeply entrenched" views that only experts with professional training should deal with dream work. "The skills involved can be identified, learned, and applied by anyone interested enough to do so," he writes in *The Variety of Dream Experience*. So let us look at the various ways we can all confront our dreams.

THE VARIETIES OF DREAMS

We advise that you do not begin to consider the content of your dreams until you have collected a respectable number of dream accounts in your journal over the period of a week or more – even several weeks if you are having difficulty recalling your dreams. Then take a preliminary overview of those accounts. You will probably soon realise, without the intervention of any expert, that most dream theories contain some truth, though none are completely true to the exclusion of all the others. So you may dream about a smoking factory chimney. Yes, this may be a phallic symbol in the terms of your dream as a whole, but otherwise, depending on the context of your own knowledge and intuition, it may be dream advice to give up smoking, or a reflection of your concerns about pollution, or the urging by your unconscious mind to bend your waking efforts to industry in some matter, or even a warning about overworking. You will know which is which, because your dreams will in the main speak to you in symbols, metaphors, puns, that over time you will begin to recognise. Certainly, their language will reflect your times and culture, but it will essentially be personal to you. This is why, in the final analysis, *only you can interpret your dreams.* In this case, familiarity can breed competence. "Dream dictionaries are dumb," states the Canadian experimental psychologist, Tore Nielson. We agree, and that is why we do not provide a list of so-called symbolic dream meanings in these pages, quite apart from the fact that it would deviate from the main concern of this book.

You will find that not all dreams are equal. Some will indeed be garbage, apparently random rehashes of the impressions of the day, but others will contain pearls of wisdom that cannot be so readily dismissed. You will see creative intelligence at work, and though it may be your own, it is from a part of you that is not only hidden away but that may contain wisdom and clarity not readily accessible to your waking ego.

Dreams as Diagnostic Tools

Some dreams will contain imagery relating to your current life activities, and this will be drawn from your personal unconscious mind. Other dreams may contain powerful, transpersonal symbols from deeper levels of the unconscious: the archetypal or mythical realm according to Jung, which belongs to humanity at large. If this is so, then your dreaming mind could be tapping into cellular memory, into your DNA. Occasionally, some other totally odd and mysterious dreams may seem unrelated in any way to your life or identifiable mythic themes. But most dreams will be diagnostic in one way or another of your present state – your life, your health, relationships, inner tensions and anxieties. Always bear this in mind when attempting to unravel a dream. You will just have to trust to your own sense and intuition as to whether the judgements you make are right for you.

Learning the Lingo

When you make your initial review of dreams in your dream journal, you may note that certain images recur at intervals. Your dream consciousness may employ a specific *lingua franca* you will have to learn. Such recurring imagery gives you an opportunity to get a "handle" on it. By comparing different dream contexts, you may be able to pick up an insistent message from your unconscious mind. You may come to see that a certain image or symbol changes its meaning or emphasis over time, depending on context and what has been happening to you in your waking life. You may also note that some dreams are only episodes in an ongoing dream saga. A dream on one night might be picked up, and expanded, developed, or improvised upon on succeeding nights, or even over following weeks. It will usually only be by considering such a set of dreams together that you will be able to get to the root of what it is they are about.

The Context of Waking Life

When you settle down to interpret a specific dream, you may find that by reference to your daytime notes in your journal the content of a dream becomes quite explicable. It is a prerequisite to check what happened in waking life in the day or days leading up to a dream. Many dreams relate to recent events. In these cases, a dream may have very easily interpretable metaphorical elements, or may even be shorn of them entirely and offer a direct reflection of daytime concerns and activities, or a commentary upon them, though from the inside. It is always worth paying heed to the inside perspective known to your unconscious mind, because often your dreams will note things that your waking self ignored or failed to see. Such missing information in your waking perception may relate to your behaviour, someone else's behaviour, or some other factor of a situation that was overlooked by your waking mind. Respect the intelligence that directs your dreams, and you will not go far wrong.

By Association

Most dreams are not amenable to direct interpretation. Most are elliptical in nature. Let us suppose that a kid you knew years back in school suddenly appears in a dream – a person out of mind until the specific dream account that recalls it. Instead of wondering about the incongruity of such a figure appearing in the dream, ask what it means. Use an associative approach. How did you feel about this person? Did you feel inferior or superior to him or her? Was there something about the person you especially admired, or detested? Did you associate the person with a particular place, time or recurring event? If so, apply the same associative thinking to the time, place or event portrayed in the dream. Eventually, you may realise that the intelligence of your dreaming mind did not put the foreign image in your dream in a literal sense, but because it held a meaning for you. It wasn't a character, but a cognitive element in the jigsaw puzzle many dreams represent. You often have to work sideways to move forward in the understanding of your dreams.

Body Messages in Dreams

In weighing up interpretative possibilities for a dream, it is very important to be aware that bodily (somatic) effects can play a significant role in generating dream imagery. P. D. Ouspensky, for example, used to have a recurring unpleasant dream in which he was struggling across a bog. He eventually found this dream was triggered by him tangling his feet in the folds of his blanket! He also ascribed dreams in which he was naked or partially dressed to a cold atmosphere in the bedroom affecting his sleeping body. Tore Neilsen has found that tightening a blood pressure cuff on the arms or legs of sleeping subjects tended to produce dreams containing "strong presences". This has led journalist George Howe Colt to drily comment that great leaders such as Hannibal, Bismarck, biblical figures, and suchlike, having powerful, prophetic dreams affecting the course of history that came not from angelic sources but because "they slept on their hand kind of funny". Patricia Garfield cites a dream in which she was taking a sweater off a baby, but it caught on the back of the infant's head and she had to pull at it. She awoke to find that she had strained a muscle during her sleep and had a severe neck pain. And many of us will have had the sort of dreams in which we are running alongside gushing streams or waterfalls only to awake and find that we need to pay an urgent call to the bathroom! In a similar way, sounds, smells and other physical stimuli in our sleeping environment can often work their way into our dreams. (Indeed, we use that fact in dream incubation.)

There are also some hints that dreams can predict illness, or at least the course of illnesses. Oliver Sacks, the neurologist and writer, famous for his book, *The Man Who Mistook His Wife for a Hat*, has found that people with multiple sclerosis, strokes or neurological damage sometimes dream of an improvement in their condition before it happens. So it may pay to scrutinise your dream journal entries with special care: the diagnostic aspect of some of your dreams may contain a warning or prognosis regarding your bodily health. Patricia Garfield, again, found that when she dreams of drooping, sickly flowers and plants, it is a reflection of her state of health, and when everything in her dream garden is blooming, so is her physical condition.

Group Exploration of Dreams

Dream study need not be a solitary occupation. You can join a dream group, or set one up, in which all its members can discuss their dreams with one another. Montague Ullman points out the process of bringing a dream into our conscious awareness is a way of "socialising" a part of our individual minds. He feels that working on dreams in a supportive and stimulating group setting is the most natural and effective context. Also, a dream might contain an unpleasant truth about us, he warns, and we may be better able to confront it in a supportive social context where trust has been established.

In a group experience, the dreamer puts forward a dream and the group members can then ask questions and offer opinions to help the dreamer clarify ideas about the dream and grasp its import. But Ullman stresses that the dreamer should always be in control of the process, and must never be pushed beyond the limits of privacy he or she has determined as being safe for them. If an associative thread is developed, it must come from the dreamer in the first instance and not other members of the group – they are there to assist, not to lead the dreamer. The dreamer's authority of his or her dream must remain paramount. If a group member explores an idea about someone else's dream, they should preface it with a phrase such as "If it were my dream..." so the actual dream remains the property of the dreamer who volunteered it to the group. All members of the group should share their dreams, even the group leader if there is one. A group leader should not impose authority on any dreamer but simply instruct in any techniques being used and handle the dynamics of the group. And enough time must be given to the often tortuous process of unravelling the meaning of a dream. It is also a good idea for a dreamer to continue working at home on a dream initially volunteered to the group, following up leads that may have emerged during the group work.

Mystery Dreams

On rare occasions, some dreams will appear to have some inexplicable elements in them, even after thorough analysis, and the dreamer should not be too reluctant about ascribing possible paranormal properties to them, even though such ideas are dismissed by our mainstream science (don't allow the consensus cultural view of reality to police your dreaming mind). We referred to paranormal dreams in an earlier chapter, and return briefly to the subject here as it holds so much potential for future study and thus many implications for the way we normally view things. It also is something that anyone studying their dreams in any depth for a long period of time is likely to encounter.

The sort of dream involved was well exemplified by Charles Dickens who recorded a dream in which he saw a woman in a red shawl with her back to him. She turned round and said: "I am Miss Napier." Dickens awoke thinking it was a "preposterous" dream as there was nothing in his experience that could have led to it; he had never seen this woman and had never heard of a Miss Napier. Yet that very evening, after he had given a reading, the woman he had seen in his dream came up to him and introduced herself as Miss Napier.

Interestingly, many leading dream researchers have come to the conclusion that telepathy in dreams seems to be a real possibility. Jung of course thought so, and so did Freud to some extent. Calvin Hall, Medard Boss, Robert Van de Castle, Montague Ullman and numerous others have similarly supported the idea. Ullman, with American psychologist Stanley Krippner, conducted the famous dream telepathy experiments in the Dream Laboratory at the Maimonides Medical Center in Brooklyn, New York. In these, randomly-selected art pictures were studied and drawn by an "agent" who "sent" the image and association of the image to a sleeping subject in another, soundproof, room who was wired to a polygraph. The effort was made every time the subject was in REM sleep. The subject would be awoken at the end of the REM period and any dreams recorded. Transcripts of these were later studied by judges for any correspondences with the art print involved. The whole range of experiments was well

Paranormal dreams often seem to involve trivial matters. As a case in point, dream subject Alan Vaughan had been watching one of his favourite writers, Kurt Vonnegut, on TV. He dreamt about the writer two nights later, and wrote to Vonnegut on 13 March 1970, describing the dream. He told Vonnegut he had seen him in a house full of children, and planning to leave on a trip to an island called Jerome. A couple of weeks later, Vonnegut replied saying, "Not bad". He explained that on the night of Vaughan's dream, he had dinner with Jerome B., the author of children's books, at which they had discussed Vonnegut's forthcoming trip to the British Isles. This case admirably demonstrates how key elements of information can be received in a dream, even if in a slightly scrambled form.

designed, with careful screening, double-blind testing, and the application of sophisticated statistics. The results proved in favour of dream telepathy, and remain as powerful evidence for it.

The keeping of a dream journal, with dated dreams, is the best way to tell if any of your dreams prove to be precognitive.

CUSTOM-MADE DREAMS

When you are reasonably competent at dream recall, and have some basic grasp of your personal dreaming grammar, you can encourage your dreaming mind to produce dreams with specific characteristics or particular functions if you so wish and are prepared to work at it. We have already touched on the process involved – incubation, the deliberate induction of a dream. We have seen that the method has been used from antiquity. A more recent, famous example of incubation is Robert Louis Stevenson's *Dr Jekyll and Mr Hyde*: the author, who had developed a considerable measure of dream control, had money trouble, so he incubated a dream to provide him with the essence of a story that would sell well! The method can work for you too.

A typical reason for incubation could be to seek an answer to some problem you are mulling over in your waking mind. Include a special request in your "Prayer to Morpheus" during your bedtime ritual. When you get into bed, summarise and write down the problem you wish to dream about in a very brief sentence, then read it out loud to yourself several times before settling down to sleep. Incubatory pleas are most successfully communicated to the unconscious mind when relaxing prior to the onset of sleep. You can, however, strengthen the bedtime process even further by repeating the incubatory phrase several times during the day: "Tonight I will receive dream advice on ---", "Tonight I will dream about ---", or whatever set of words you choose.

While incubated dreams can appear quickly, perhaps on the night of the first induction, experience indicates that it can take up to several weeks for your waking message to get through to your unconscious mind and the first dream that deals with your specific incubation to appear. So you must be prepared to be persistent. Also, you have to develop the skill to interpret material in a dream that may be dealing with your request, always remembering that dream information can be elliptical and/or associative, so that on awakening the desired dream may seem to be irrelevant to the reasons for your induction process. But casually thinking about it on and off over the course of the day may provide associations that allow you to see that an insight was indeed provided.

How you pose your incubatory request is also important. Highly specific questions about what job you should pursue, or who you should marry, are unlikely to produce the kind of answer you seek – you can't really expect placards to pop up in a dream saying "yes" or "no" to a narrow question. While dreams can sometimes supply a very precise, if symbolic answer, to some specific request on an intellectual or mathematical problem, as we saw in earlier chapters, it is usually wiser to seek advice as to the dynamics surrounding a situation, problem or decision, especially when it is a personal matter. To put that another way, instead of asking "Should I take this job?", it would be better to pose the question along the lines of, "What should I do about my work situation?". Who knows, you might receive dream advice about going into some line of work you hadn't even thought about consciously. Give your inner consultant full rein. But a word of caution: treat dream responses as only one factor to weigh up in making a decision about anything. The real value of dream incubation is that some aspect of yourself you had not placed much value on, or some dimension to a situation you hadn't consciously noticed, can be illuminated by a dream, thus allowing you to make a more balanced overall decision.

For us here and now, the most important form of dream incubation concerns how to induce a lucid dream. It is to that specific task we now turn.

CHAPTER 4

Awake Within a Dream

YOU may have had one or more spontaneous lucid dreams, but if you want to be able to have them more frequently, and more robustly, then you will need to work at it. By putting some of the information in the previous chapter into action for some weeks you will be in a good starting position, as you will be much more in touch with your dream life. You can let your "dream-awareness" nights transform into the nights on which you practice the development of lucid dreaming. As with any other skill, do not be discouraged if it takes a little time to become proficient. The first lucid dream is the most difficult one, and so if you do get the gift of an early lucid dream experience, or if you have had a spontaneous one in the recent past, you are already over the first hurdle. But even if this is not the case, if you diligently practice your chosen methods from those presented in this chapter, you will learn to achieve lucidity in your dreams.

The Nature of Lucid Dreams

Although lucidity is usually accessed through normal dreaming, do not confuse lucid dreams themselves with vivid dreams. *They are a state of altered consciousness in their own right*, distinct from even the most vivid of normal dreams. There are, nevertheless, varying degrees of lucidity, ranging from a fleeting flash of conscious awareness within an otherwise ordinary dream to "high" lucid dreams of apparent total realism containing astounding detail. There is a whole set of gradations in between. Lucidity is directly proportional to the clarity of your awareness within a dream: the more fully conscious and aware you become within a dream, so will the dream scenery take on greater richness, reality and depth accordingly. Alan Worsley has noted that the level of lucidity can vary even in the same dream. At its best, lucid dreaming creates a verisimilitude of physical, waking reality – and sometimes even more intense than that.

You have to find ways to alert yourself within a normal dream that you are dreaming, but the level of consciousness that has to be achieved requires a fine balancing act between falling back into unaware dreaming, or waking up from sleep altogether. It is virtually a form of yoga that can only be learned through trial and error. Emotional control, even a measure of detachment, is necessary to maintain a lucid dream experience for any length of time. If you become too excited, you wake up; if too absorbed in the content of the lucid dream, there is a risk of slipping back into ordinary, non-aware dreaming. "Like crossing a narrow board, you must keep your balance to avoid falling one way or the other," Garfield advises.

Lucid dreaming can be accessed in any REM period in a sleep cycle, but the very best time is in the longer and more energetic REM periods occurring an hour or two before you normally awake. Keith Hearne states flatly that lucid dreams are essentially "a phenomenon of the second half of the night". But lucid dreaming can also be accessed in the midst of hypnogogic imagery at the onset of sleep, as we shall see later. At the other end of the sleep cycle, awakening, there are other opportunities to gain dream lucidity, as we shall also learn.

There is no problem in remembering lucid dreams – you can recall them just as well as you remember events in waking life. This is because the conscious self is involved both in waking awareness and in lucid dreaming. Nevertheless, we advise that you keep a written record of your lucid dreams just as you do of your normal dreams.

The perceptual quality of lucid dreams is noteworthy. In the way that we can distinguish subtle differences between, say, a photographic print and a newspaper photograph, so too does a lucid dream have a specific visual texture. There is usually a prevailing clarity of light and a translucency to colours almost as if they were illuminated from within. Lucid dream lighting tends to have that sort of crystalline purity one might get a hint of on a crisp, clear sunlit winter morning, with ice crystals glinting sharply and the white snow and frost vividly contrasting with a flawless azure sky. In one dream, Patricia Garfield felt that light emanated from inside her own eyes, and it is true that the lucid dreamer can often be particularly aware of the dream-body's eyes. Keith Hearne, for instance, noted tightness around the "eyes" with which he gazed on a lucid dream scene, and we would say that it feels rather akin to putting on a pair of eyeglasses that are not quite the right prescription – there is a very mild sense of optical strain. This seems to be related to the nature of lucid dream consciousness in that to maintain the necessary level of lucidity a way of "seeing" within the dream needs to be evolved.

Virtual versions of all sensory modalities can operate in lucid dreams, though not necessarily all together in a single dream. Although the visual sense usually predominates, smell, taste, touch and hearing are all able to make their appearances in the lucid dream state. In a few rare cases, it is possible to have one or more of these sensory modes as the dominant ones.

In even in the most realistic lucid dream, however, words on a page tend to be elusive. The dreamer might be able to read a page of writing quite readily, but when the book is looked at again the words will have changed in some way. A similar effect is noticeable on digital clocks seen in lucid dreams.

Then there is the issue of how dreamers image themselves in lucid dreams. In reality, there is no need to have a body at all in the lucid state. One could simply be what the German lucid dream researcher, Paul Tholey, called an "ego-point" just floating around or entering into dream characters at will. But we are so used to carrying an image of ourselves in waking life that the habit usually persists into the lucid dream state.

Mary Arnold-Forster wrote accounts of numerous lucid dreams she had in which sensory effects other than the visual were noticeable. These were sometimes quite subtle. In one dream she was motoring through deep valleys as dusk was beginning to fall. She detected "the faint scent, cold, clean and unmistakable, that belongs to valley mist". She also complained of not been able to find a confectioner in waking life who could produce the flavour of an entrancing green candy she tasted in a dream!

But because it is an image, it can be changed and distorted. Garfield has reported that she has appeared in various guises in her lucid dreams, including as a man and as a half-animal, half-human figure. J.H. Whiteman, a South African researcher, found himself as a girl in one lucid dream, and remarked on the detailed difference of bodily sensibility he experienced. Alan Worsley has conducted some particularly bizarre experiments. On a number of occasions he has passed his dream-body's forearms through each other, experiencing a "dragging" sensation. On another occasion, he was able to sink his dream-body's hands into his dream head, inside of which he felt the tissue of a brain.

A LUCID DREAMING SUPERMARKET

We have given each of the lucid dream induction "packages" described below a "brand name". Look at all these packages as if you were browsing along a supermarket shelf. Pick out those that have an initial appeal for you, and leave the others until another visit if necessary.

The Days of our Lives

It has been noticed by several researchers that busy days in which you meet a lot of people, do considerable travelling or are involved in numerous activities, seem to provide nights particularly susceptible to lucid dreaming. In her *Pathways to Ecstasy,* Patricia Garfield notes that after such days "I might also be tired, anxious, exhausted, sick or feeling fine, but I am usually stimulated with many activities, ideas, and people."

Life is But a Dream

One can begin preparation for the planned night of lucidity during the day, and every day. Whatever you are doing, ask yourself: "Am I awake or asleep? Is this reality, or is it a dream?" In other words, develop a habit of testing your state of consciousness until it becomes an automatic reflex. It can then carry over into your dream life, and consequently provide a critical cue for lucidity. Paul Tholey suggested that the question should be asked at least five to ten times a day. You can also programme yourself to ask the question at set times of the day, such as when coming home from work, or by setting a wristwatch alarm. You might even write a cue card that says "Is this a dream?" and put it in your wallet, pocket, on your desk at work and so forth, where it will give you occasional, unexpected reminders to test your state of consciousness.

This method originates in Tibetan dream yoga, where the novice is instructed to think continuously that "all things are of the substance of dreams". It is a powerful technique. As Stephen LaBerge has remarked, how can you expect to ask yourself if a dream is a dream when you are in one, if you never question your mental state in waking life?

A-scent Into Lucidity

All the lucid dream incubation methods use memory as the main ingredient in one way or another, whether it is to form a habitual action, employ visualisation, or to try to carry an intention over into the sleeping state, as with normal dream incubation. A powerful adjunct to this process can be the use of scent. We have all had the experience of smelling an odour that immediately conjures an image of something from earlier in our lives. The olfactory sense connects to the limbic system, where the hippocampus interprets smells and helps form memories, and where the amygdala is thought to play a role in emotions. Smell is therefore a highly suitable sense to use as a mnemonic aid. And scent can reach into dreams. This was shown by Saint-Denys. He constantly used a certain perfume while he was visiting a particular holiday location for two weeks. He used it only at this place. Some months later, the perfume was applied to his pillow during the night. Sure enough, it induced a dream of the vacation spot. In more recent experimentation, Alan Worsley found that odours influenced the content of his lucid dreams, and that differentiation of scents was possible in the lucid dream state. There were some anecdotal reports in the 1980s that scent had been used for cueing subjects for lucid dreaming while they were in the REM state, and there is ongoing research into the effects of fragrances on sleep in general.

The power of scent is associative. That being so, you can select a fragrance specifically to accompany a chosen induction method. For example, when asking yourself if you are dreaming in the day, sniff the selected fragrance from a bottle of essential oil or perfume at the same time. Or, burn a particular incense when you do your bedtime incubation (this would be best as an essential oil, as that can be both vaporised as an incense and sprinkled on the pillow as a fragrance). The scent can act like a "carrier wave", reminding you in your dreams of the induction or critical awareness you have been working on to trigger you into lucidity. It is of course important that the scent used has no other associations for you, and that you ensure no other smell is involved when you do your incubation.

Oiling the Dream Machine

Essential oils can be used in other ways than solely for scent. Some have specific sedative and hypnotic characteristics, as noted earlier with regard to Clary Sage. You might also experiment with classic sleep and dream producers such as lavender, rose, myrrh, and patchouli. You might mix your own dreaming blends (and some are available commercially). One is frankincense with myrrh and sandalwood, or another suggestion would be a mix of equal parts of Clary Sage, rose otto, jasmine and vanilla. Also, the essential oil of nutmeg is available, and this can be inhaled by sprinkling a few drops on the pillow or bedclothes. (As advised previously, if you apply oils directly to the skin, make sure they are suspended in a "carrier oil" such as grapeseed, almond or jojoba. Only one or two drops of essential oil per tablespoon of carrier oil are necessary, and the mixture should be stirred or shaken before use to ensure that the essential oil is dispersed in the carrier. Do not ingest the oils. Essential oils used for these purposes should be unadulterated and of therapy standard.)

The Power of Place

Memory and place are curiously linked. This was recognised in the classical world by a system called "the method of loci" ('method of places'). In this memorising technique, a person commits to memory the visualised layout of a building, or any geographic location that provides a suitable number of separate spots, like rooms, or houses and shops down a street, or even islands in a bay. If the person wants to remember a list of items, he or she "walks" in their mind through the visualised locale, and mentally assigns each item on the list to a separate spot within the imagined scene. Each item becomes visually linked in the imagination with the visualised spot. When the time comes to retrieve the list of items, the person simply "walks" back through the memorised locale "seeing" the items that had been "deposited" earlier in their various places. It is a proven method for recalling information that is otherwise difficult to retain in one's mind. We can use this mnemonic power of place in our quest for lucid dream induction.

Think of a place you frequent most days. A good choice would be the kitchen in your home. This is for three reasons: you visit the place a lot, it is convenient, and in a study of a hundred lucid dreams Keith Hearne found that familiar locations like the kitchen figured by far the most often as interior settings in lucid dreams. Actually, there is a fourth reason – you are likely to have a fridge in the kitchen. So write boldly in felt tip on a slip of paper or card "LUCID IN THE SKY WITH DIAMONDS", and fix it to the refrigerator door with a few of those little fridge magnets. Day in, day out, as you pass through the kitchen or busy yourself there, catch sight of the note on the fridge, and think of (or hum, whistle or sing) the tune of the Beatles' song, "Lucy in the Sky with Diamonds". Prime your dreaming mind by incorporating into your incubation procedures an intent to visit the kitchen in your dreams and of becoming lucid when you do so. It will be only a matter of time until either the kitchen figures in your dreams, or some associated image – jewellery, frozen wastelands, glittering ice crystals in the sky, the Beatles, the tune – does so. Then, unless you have a particularly stubborn dreaming mind, you will be triggered into lucidity.

All Change

A lucid dream can sometimes be triggered simply by changing your sleeping arrangements. So try a shift from a mattress to a water bed, or go to sleep on the floor or a sofa for a night. Make it part of a special induction procedure. If you are really keen and adventurous, you might even arrange a fairly uncomfortable sleeping situation, so you will tend to wake quite frequently during the night.

Take a Deep Breath

Little modern research has been done on breathing with regard to lucid dreaming. In Tibetan dream yoga, "pot-shaped" breathing is recommended. In this, you expel the used air in the lungs using three exhalations, then inhale taking the air into the bottom of the lungs while raising the diaphragm slightly, making the distended chest and abdomen rounded and similar to the shape of an earthenware pot, and holding as long as possible. This is repeated seven times. Another type of breathing that can cause mind states similar to lucid dreaming is hyperventilation, rapid shallow breathing, which psychologist Stanislav Grof has incorporated into his "psychotropic" breathwork technique. However, this form of breathing can be dangerous, leading all too easily to blackouts, and should not be undertaken without expert supervision.

Take Your Positions

As far as posture goes, lucid dreamer extraordinaire, Alan Worsley, reckons he lucid dreams best when he sleeps in a face-down position with his forearms under his chest and fists to his cheeks. This sounds uncomfortable, and Worsley admits that the position sometimes makes his arms go numb, but is very effective for him. When not sleeping specifically to have lucid dreams, he lies on his side. Because research in this area is as sparse as in breathing techniques, you will have to experiment. Try out various sleeping postures, and when you achieve lucidity, make a note of the sleeping position you had adopted.

Dream with a Plan

When you incubate a dream, plan to do something specific in it, and tell yourself that this will trigger lucidity for you. Garfield suggests flying, as that in itself often leads automatically to lucidity in a dream. As part of the induction procedure, spend some time observing birds in flight, read about birds, aircraft, levitating yogis – anything that carries the message. Tholey recommended planning to carry out a simple action in a dream, such as slowly waving an arm or looking at your hands.

Electric Dreams

Today's researchers have sought to invent electronic ways of inducing lucid dreaming and associated mental states. There have been some successes, but no panaceas. Even if you use an electronic aid, it will not automatically confer lucidity in your dreams, and you will need to work with it as you would with any other method. A disadvantage is that electronic aids are of course more expensive than using psychological induction methods. For some people, though, the use of an instrument may appeal.

One of the most widely-used devices is the NovaDreamer, developed by Laberge's Lucidity Institute in California (www.lucidity.com). This ingenious instrument consists of a lightweight, padded eye mask fitted with a tiny computerised electronic circuit and red LEDs in the eye positions. Infrared sensors detect the rapid eye movements indicative of REM sleep, and this sets off a programmable selection of light and sound cues which can enter the wearer's dreams, hopefully triggering lucidity.

Keith Hearne has used monitored breathing as a basis for a possible lucid dream device. Sessions with prototypes did apparently prove successful.

ENTERING THE TWILIGHT ZONE

After your daytime preparations and bedtime inductions, you come to sleep onset itself. You need to become acutely aware of this hypnogogic transitional state between waking and sleeping. It is a doorway, a "crack between the worlds" in which access to lucidity can be made. The hypnogogic stage is a "warp" between two states of consciousness. A gap, a no-man's land. The hypnogogic warp can be opened out and extended into a phase of consciousness in its own right.

Hypnogogic lucid dreams – what Van Eeden called "initial dreams" – occur in NREM Stage 1 sleep, and so tend to last for shorter times and with less volitional control than full-bodied REM lucid dreaming later in the sleep cycle, but they are lucid dreams nevertheless. Ouspensky described one of his experiences of hypnogogic images as "golden sparks and dots" that transformed into a net with regular meshes, then "the golden net was transformed into the helmets of the Roman soldiers". At the same time he heard a pulsation like the measured tread of a marching detachment. Most of us will recall similar brief flashes of imagery – geometric patterns, faces, scenes, and brief snatches of sound like a ringing bell while falling asleep. All too often, however, this all passes by rapidly and before we know it, we are waking up in the morning. Some people, indeed, are hardly aware of the hypnogogic stage, thinking that they just pass straight into sleep. Because of these tendencies, there are two tricks the aspiring lucid dreamer needs to master in this twilight zone: (i) becoming aware of and slowing down the process of falling asleep, and (ii) being able to carry a thread of cognition or visualisation across the hypnogogic threshold. We present here a range of exercises for use in the hypnogogic state. Select as required.

Finding your Warp Factor

If you can slow down the process of falling asleep, and become more attuned to the darting hypnogogic imagery, you will almost certainly experience fleeting moments of lucidity as a function of the state itself. It is probably the most automatic way to achieve lucidity. One way of slowing down the process of falling asleep is simply by forcing yourself to be observant as you get increasingly drowsy – let your body go to sleep while trying to keep your mind awake. Although this is easier said than done, the fact is that the more you attempt it, the more familiar you will become with the state and easier you will find managing it to be. A delicate mental balancing act is required. Your bedtime condition is important. You need to be tired enough to fall asleep, but not so exhausted that you "zonk out" before having a chance to put the brakes on a little. So do not attempt this work if you are overly tired, or if you have had a big evening meal or have imbibed too much alcohol.

Ann Faraday has suggested a technique originally put forward by the astral projector, Sylvan Muldoon (see following chapter), that helps you identify the moment of sleep onset. It uses the fact that muscle tone decreases in sleep. She suggests that as you settle to sleep, you prop your arm up in a comfortable, vertical position, balanced on its elbow so that it will fall as sleep kicks in and your muscles become slack. It will help to keep you in that all-important warp between wakefulness and sleep, and become familiar with it.

Countdown

Stephen LaBerge has put forward a simple technique for the hypnogogic transition. As you fall asleep, you start counting to yourself "One, I'm dreaming; two, I'm dreaming" and so on. At some point in your countdown to sleep there is a good probability that you'll be mentally saying something like "thirty-nine, I'm dreaming..." and you actually will be dreaming. You will have carried a thread of awareness over into your dream from waking consciousness. LaBerge calls such attempts WILDs: Wake-Initiated Lucid Dreams, and contrasts them to DILDs, Dream-Initiated Lucid Dreams.

Marking the Spot

A traditional Tibetan dream yoga technique is to visualise a black, white or coloured dot or a lotus blossom while falling asleep. There are numerous versions, and within the belief system of Tibetan Buddhism they all have special meanings. For our more secular requirements, we suggest that you try a technique asserted to by the neuro-anthropologist, Charles Laughlin, in which, as you enter the hypnogogic stage, you visualise as strongly as you can a red, pill-like spot glowing like an LED either between the eyebrows or in the throat behind and slightly below your larynx, while mentally or audibly intoning an "AHHHH" sound. If you can carry this visualisation into the dream state the thread of consciousness might come along with it.

Other Dimensions

When you are settled in bed and feeling drowsy, take a look at a book of those complex repetitive patterns called stereographs that can suddenly transform into 3D pictures if you focus on them in the right way. Practice this as sleep approaches. If you fall asleep and the book falls, it will awake you. Carry on until it falls again. And so on. When the image you are focusing on flips into 3D, be conscious of the muscular control your eyes are employing, and at the same time, ponder on where the space has come from – after all, the pattern you are using is on a flat page. What is space? How can you produce it like this? Keep at this exercise on the very borderline of sleep for as long as you possibly can before finally falling fast asleep. If you keep switching in and out of sleep, and in and out of that special 3D focus, with the hypnogogic flux flooding around the edges of your awareness and the conundrum of space on your mind, you will make yourself highly prone to dream lucidity. You will be storming a dimensional door.

Radio Control

You can use your audio sense in much the same way. Turn on your bedside radio, just loud enough to be intelligible. Tune to a talk show or a news broadcast, not music. As you fall asleep, concentrate hard on following what is being said as you drift into sleep, using it as a thread to keep conscious attention running as deeply as possible into the hypnogogic state.

Down the Ancient Passageway

In Figure 9 you can see the depiction of a dark passageway leading off toward a bright light. This is a very powerful picture because it images a deep pattern or programme in the human brain scientists call an "entoptic form" (Chapter 1). Many people who have a near-death experience (NDE) report the sensation of floating down a tunnel towards a light, and a similar effect is frequently noted in out-of-body

Fig. 9: An ancient passage, as old as the human mind. Imagine yourself floating through it toward the light...

Fig. 10: A "tunnel" of trees is also an image that can act like the entoptic passage leading to trance consciousness.

experiences (OBEs). This tunnel-like image is a reflex of the in-built mental programme for falling into trance (of which the NDE, the OBE and the lucid dream are various forms), and is as old as human consciousness. It is described in ancient and tribal societies worldwide, and was even depicted in one of the strange paintings by the medieval artist, Hieronymus Bosch. Numerous lucid dreamers have also reported the image. Patricia Garfield has particularly noted that one often encounters a passage of some kind, a doorway, tunnel, tube or gap, and when the lucid dreamer goes through, there is another scene entirely. Whiteman recalled lying in bed and apparently awake, when suddenly he saw a visual opening with a circular boundary. Inside he saw a scene in bright sunlight. He found himself passing through the opening, and felt that it represented a gulf between two spheres of existence. Worsley found himself lying in a dark tunnel of what seemed to be polished mahogany. He slid through it feet first and was propelled into a bright scene in which he saw a procession of people. A lucid dream began for British psychologist Susan Blackmore by her travelling rapidly along a few feet above a road, over which tree branches arched like a tunnel.

By concentrating on the passage theme you can actually prime that inner programme to "click in" when you fall asleep or, later, at some point in a dream. So spend five to ten minutes gazing at one of the images here in Figures 9-11 with unbroken attention frequently just before falling to sleep. Perhaps make an enlarged photocopy of one of them and fix it where you can see it easily when comfortably in bed, and imagine yourself floating through or along that ancient passageway, as old as the human mind itself. When you have finished this visualisation session, immediately turn off the light and settle to sleep. A few days or weeks of doing this will make it highly probable that such a tunnel image, pathway, doorway or similar portal will start to appear in your dreams. You will begin to move into and along it. This is the moment when the recognition factor that "I'm dreaming!" can be activated. Go with the movement through the passage or portal , allowing your conscious, critical

Fig. 11: Narrow, straight pathways are yet another type of image that can act like the entoptic tunnel leading to the magical country beyond.

faculties to grow as you fly along. You will burst out of the far end of the tunnel or pathway and find yourself fully conscious but in a remarkable lucid dream otherworld.

Sweet Dreams

Let us look at some ways of achieving lucidity while actually in the fully asleep, dreaming part of the sleep cycle.

On the Lookout

In a survey of one hundred lucid dreams, Hearne found that the single most important trigger is the observation by the dreamer of some kind of incongruity or inconsistency in a dream. This can take many forms. For example, you might find yourself in familiar surroundings in a dream, but notice that something is missing, wrong or out of place, or you may be walking around a house you lived in years ago, and suddenly realise that you no longer live there.

Some dreams are "pre-lucid" in nature, in which the dreamer is alerted to the point of lucidity. Pre-lucidity often involves a vigorous sense of movement – you may be dreaming that you are running, walking briskly, jumping, leaping, or very busy with some task or journey. Normal flying dreams are strongly pre-lucid. Tunnels, in whatever form, are a sure sign that lucidity is hovering near, as we have already discussed.

Recurring images in dreams are a very useful gift from the dreaming mind. Use your dream journal to identify these, if you can't think of any without prompting. They are what LaBerge calls "dreamsigns". Identify them, write a list of them, and encourage their appearance by invoking them in bedtime incubation. You can thus prepare yourself for their appearance in your dreams. They are friendly reminders that can nudge you awake within a dream.

The Useful Nightmare

Anxiety or emotional stress within a dream is another powerful trigger for initiating lucidity. In this regard, the nightmare can be an ally. Celia Green observes that people who have a recurrent nightmare sometimes report a learning effect. The familiarity of the nightmare, however scary it might be, reminds them that this is a situation in which they can realise that they are dreaming. The type of lucidity resulting from this tends to be very brief, because the sufferer of the nightmare wakes up. While this can be thought of as an escape, the trick is to use the nightmare situation as a platform for lucidity, and to realise before awakening occurs that there is no need to be fearful of any dream image – the images of the nightmare are only your own thoughtforms. Stand up to your nightmare in the full knowledge that it cannot harm you.

Sensational

There are various "physical" sensations at the onset of, and sometimes accompanying, lucid dreams that can come to be recognised by the persistent lucid dreamer. They can often start in a pre-lucid dream, and offer yet another signal to alert the dreamer to lucidity.

If you are having a non-lucid flying dream, then the sensations of flight or floating become obvious haptic mnemonics, as these sensations are very common in lucid dreams. This alone is likely to trigger lucidity. In the case of a tunnel-type image, a typical feeling is not only of travelling through it but of an increasing speed as you do so. You often hurtle your way into lucidity! Also, research has indicated that when in a lucid dream, there seems to be a relationship between apparent movement of the dream-body and the maintenance of lucidity. Lucid dreams without motion occurring somewhere in their fabric tend to fade away. This might be why busy dreams, and ones containing running and other movements tend to harbour pre-lucid potential. Do not be alarmed if weird sounds and apparent vibrations accompany entry into lucidity.

OH WHAT A BEAUTIFUL MORNING!

It is not only preparation before going to sleep, and techniques attempted during dreaming itself, that can assist the production of lucid dreams: there are methods that can be employed at the other, waking, end of the sleep cycle too. These are the most effective of all lucid dream induction methods, in fact. In a normal night's sleep, the longest REM cycle is in the hour or two before one wakes up, say the period from around 6 am. That is when many people have their lucid dreams.

Wake Up to Lucidity

Stephen LaBerge's Lucidity Institute has found that an extremely effective way to promote lucidity is to set your alarm about two hours before you normally wake up. (Obviously, only try this method when you don't have to go to work the next day!). The Institute suggests getting up and conducting some activity for two hours, reading, watching TV, or whatever it might be, then going back to sleep at the time you would normally be waking up. So if you usually awake at, say, 7 am, set the alarm to 5 am, and return to bed at 7 am then sleep for a couple of hours. You will fall straight back into a torrent of REM sleep as if it had been dammed up by the early alarm call. Because you'll be falling quickly from waking directly into REM sleep, you will be more able to retain your critical faculties than when you drift off at the beginning of a night's sleep. We can attest to the effectiveness of this technique. In our experience, it yields around a seventy percent success rate. Further, we have found that it isn't really necessary to get up and be awake for a full two hours. When the early alarm rings, you can read in bed for just 15-30 minutes, then fall back to sleep, and the method seems to work just as well.

MILD

LaBerge developed a method called "Mnemonic Induction of Lucid Dreams" that makes use of the abundant REM activity in the latter period of the sleep cycle. Basically, he advises that when you awake spontaneously from a dream in the early morning you should go over the dream in your mind several times until you have memorised it. Then, as you lay in bed returning to sleep, impress on yourself that the next time you dream, you want to recognise that you're dreaming. You visualise yourself back in the dream you have rehearsed, but this time picturing yourself realising that you are dreaming it. You go over this as many times as you can before you fall asleep once more. LaBerge says that if all goes well, you should find yourself lucid in another dream, whether or not it is like the dream you awoke from.

REM Surfing

Ouspensky noted that after waking from normal sleep, he would again close his eyes and begin to doze, while keeping his mind on some image or thought. He frequently found that this would encourage lucid dreams. You can do likewise. Choose a morning when you don't have to get up for work or have any particular commitment, and can awake naturally from sleep in your own good time. Stay in bed after waking, and doze off again, using Ouspensky's suggestion, or one of the hypnogogic techniques already described, or just being attentive to the imagery you see. You will tend to surface to wakefulness every so often, but let yourself drift back yet again. Once you get the hang of this REM surfing, you will find you can dip into and out of lucid dreams over quite prolonged periods. One of the present authors has made intermittent lucidity occur for over forty minutes at a time in this manner. This method is also known as "REM re-entry", and is an exceptionally effective lucid dreaming technique.

Morning Glory, Afternoon Delight

Naps provide excellent opportunities for employing lucid dream induction techniques. In fact, LaBerge considers them to be optimal for entering into lucid dreaming. While afternoon naps are fine, morning naps are particularly useful. This is because REM propensity and intensity are both near their peak in the morning, and biological rhythms are generally favourable. One method is to take a nap about two hours after your usual waking time. From several studies, LaBerge and colleagues found lucid dreams were, overall, ten times more likely to occur in naps than in normal nightly sleep.

Lucid Dream Activities

So. You find yourself in a lucid dream. Now that you are there, what do you do? Twiddle your dream-body's thumbs? Hardly – too much will be happening. Lucid dreaming is truly as Patricia Garfield states in her *Creative Dreaming*, "one of the most exciting experiences a person can have". Nevertheless, it is worth considering some advice and a few technical points.

Tourist of the Otherworld

We advise that for your first several lucid dreams, you don't try to do anything too much. Just look and learn. Get the hang of the lucid dream world. Be a tourist in it. The more familiar you become with it, and the mental discipline you need to exercise while in it, the easier it will be for you to enter the state again. Do not make any early attempts at dream control. If push comes to shove, ask for "guidance" and see what transpires. Rely on the ages-old wisdom of your dreaming brain.

A Question of Control

The main reasons for attempting to control or manipulate a lucid dream is for experimentation of one kind or another, or for general fun and games. The golden rule is to not interfere too much with your lucid dreams. They are powerful mental theatre, full of metaphor and information, and the value of that information is that your waking mind can directly access it but without having generated it. You are receiving news from elsewhere. Value it. But, inevitably, being human, you will want to try manipulation at some point.

The first thing you will learn is that unless you are a very experienced lucid dreamer, control is not so easy. Ouspensky noted that usually he only gave the first impetus towards a change, after which a dream would develop "as if it were by its own accord". He was sometimes astonished at the unexpected and startling turns his lucid dreams would take.

There are ways of manipulation that are likely to be more successful than others. So, for example, if you want to change the current lucid dream scenery don't try to do it wholesale by an act of sheer willpower; instead, get on a lucid dream bus or other vehicle and simulate travel to the desired location, or, as is more usual in lucid dreams, fly there yourself. Generally in a lucid dream, try to make small, incremental additions or alterations. This is especially true of lighting. If you are in a dark scene, for instance, the dreaming mind seems to need a short time lag to increase brightness by any significant amount.

Tholey noted that the scenery in a lucid dream can be quite dependent on the emotional and mental state of the dreamer. By controlling your own state, you can influence and change the scenery, and, in particular, other dream characters. You can also cause effects simply by saying what you want "out loud" in the dream, and let its own mechanism accommodate the wish in its own way, as Ouspensky similarly observed.

There is one way to make sudden, large scenic changes in a lucid dream, though, and that is to cover your dream-body's

On one dream occasion, Ouspensky found himself in a windowless room. He was looking at a black kitten and suddenly realised he was dreaming. He decided to turn the kitten into a large white dog. This duly appeared, but at the same time a wall of the dream room dissolved to disclose a mountainous landscape. Ouspensky wondered why it had appeared, and then dimly recalled that he had seen a large white dog in such a landscape long ago. The animal had brought its memory context along with it. The ecology of the mind is complex beyond our conscious knowledge.

eyes with your dream-body's hands. When you uncover your eyes, you'll be in another setting. Care is needed in using this method, because it has been found to lead to false awakenings: you cover your eyes, you open them, and you find yourself lying in bed, thinking that you have awoken.

Take it slowly, and build up your skills, and you will eventually achieve considerable control. If you find you often have unpleasant situations in your lucid dreams, LaBerge advises that you try to control yourself rather than the scenery directly – control your habitual reactions to things, and the scenery will improve. This is why lucid dreaming can be so helpful to your waking life.

Keeping the Show on the Road

The other, more important reason for lucid dream manipulation is to prolong the period of lucidity. You can usually tell when a lucid dream is about to end because the visual aspect of the dream starts to lose its characteristic vividness, the powerful three-dimensional quality similarly diminishes, and the field of view constricts.

A classic way of prolonging lucidity is to look at your dream-body's hands – the already-mentioned Castaneda technique. A variation on this is to rub the hands together vigorously. Achieving a sense of movement and friction is important. Looking at the ground is another possibility: one of the present authors did this on one occasion to stabilise a lucid dream, and saw a rain puddle showing the dream-body's reflection in it. Another favoured method is to start spinning when the lucid dream is about to fade or break up. Spin your dream-body like a top. This speed of spin is important, as a sense of movement generally helps maintain lucidity. Keep spinning, with your dream-body's arms outstretched, until you are in a vivid new dream scene, or awake. If you awake, check that it is not a false awakening.

One of the things you shouldn't do is to become too emotionally over-involved with a lucid dream. Remember it is your inner theatre, however real it appears. Don't get too excited, too frightened, too alarmed, too angry, too randy, too anything. A little, yes; too much, no. Again, good training for waking life. Also, most lucid dream experts warn against fixing your eyes for too long on something in a lucid dream. This will stop the REM action which, as we noted earlier, accompanies dreaming.

THE DENIZENS OF DREAMLAND

One of the strongest, and strangest, aspects of lucid dreams is the other characters you are likely to meet in them. This can be such a powerful experience that your first contact can cause you to awake. Do not underestimate the power of these figures. It can shock. Ouspensky remarked that in his lucid dreams he saw between ten and twenty people he had known at various stages in his life, and he noticed that "the style of each man was kept throughout to the smallest detail". Your lucid dream people can be those you know in waking life, living people, dead people, and sometimes you are likely to meet composite characters. Tholey observed that lucid dream characters can give the impression of having minds of their own. They speak and behave logically, perform amazing cognitive feats, and express in their behaviour distinct purposes and feelings. You can have some of the best conversations of your life with them. If you meet characters in successive dreams, they will recall your earlier meetings, they will act as if they remember what transpired. If you try to fix them with a stare, however, they will avert their eyes, assume jerky eye movements, pull something over their eyes like a hood, or take other evasive actions. Some of them you will make your friends and allies in the dreamworld, others you will stay wary of.

If you find yourself in an uninhabited lucid dream scene (you are likely to experience many fabulous landscapes with no people present) and want to meet someone, try to avoid making them appear out of thin air. Follow Van Eeden's example and call for them to appear. Or you could conjure up a phone to call them, open a door, look behind a rock or tree or round a corner for them.

The appearance of non-human entities is rare in lucid dreaming, but it can happen. In his lucid dreams, Van Eeden occasionally encountered non-human beings that had no intrinsic sex, being able to appear as male or female. They tended to be aggressive, obscene or impertinent, and to have a certain plasticity. He described one as being slippery, shining, limp and cold like a living corpse. Another changed its face repeatedly, making grimaces as it did so. When attacked or surrounded by these entities, Van Eeden seems to have had a great time bellowing at them and calling on the Almighty, creating whips out of thin air to flog them with, and generally belabouring the creatures. He was not afraid when he could actually see these weird beings – they only made him uneasy when out of sight. In fact, he admitted to always feeling "thoroughly refreshed, cheered up and entirely serene and calm" after one of his battles with them. Perhaps we all need to confront our demons from time to time, and clear them out with the gusto Van Eeden displayed!

EXPERIMENTING

Once you have oriented yourself in the world of lucid dreaming, and have gained a measure of control, the potential number of experiments you can attempt is limitless. One would be to make use of the powerful characters you will meet. You can ask them what they represent in the dream, which aspect of yourself. Ask them what information they bring, what news they wish to impart to you. You can try to sort out personal, psychological attitudes that you know are causing you problems. As Keith Harary and Pamela Weintraub comment, you can trade places with characters in your lucid dreams to gain even more direct insight into the significance of their presence. Both you and they are only images in a lucid dream, so such things are possible.

Fig. 12: Various lucid dreamers and out-of-body experients have reported occasionally encountering unpleasant, grimacing, "slippery and limp" entities. Remember they are constructions of your own mind and cannot physically harm you.

You can "call" family members, friends, or partners, and work out problems with them, or try out different ways of giving someone a difficult message, and test out reactions. You can even conjure up board members you have to go before shortly and rehearse your interview! You can similarly rehearse a speech, a musical solo – even sporting activities. All in all, there is no waking life situation that the lucid dreamer cannot simulate, rehearse and improve upon.

As lucid dreaming seems to be able to tap into psycho-physical mechanisms, you may even be able to effect personal health care activities. Harary and Weintraub suggest conjuring forth a lucid dream therapist who can help you manage your health. This dream person will embody all your memories and experiences of both your conscious and unconscious mind, and will have access to the most intimate details of your life. It will also have knowledge of psycho-physical processes that are not apparent to your waking ego. But Harary and Weintraub warn that your inner therapist cannot be guaranteed to give you flawless advice, so always rationally evaluate your lucid dream therapy session in the cool light of day.

We saw in an earlier chapter that lucid dreaming can be a terrific vehicle for paranormal experimentation. If you wish to test out telepathy, it is again best to work it into the logic of the dream. For example, if you want to try to communicate to a distant person, use a lucid dream telephone, or open a lucid dream door in order to talk to them. Don't talk aimlessly, exchange specific items of information that you can later check when you meet the person in waking life. Hearne cites the case of a woman who spoke with a friend on the telephone in a lucid dream. The friend was thousands of miles away in waking life. The friend said he had been ill, and described the symptoms. It later transpired that the friend had indeed been ill with those very symptoms. Overall, though, Hearne's research on parapsychology and lucid dreams has shown mixed results.

You can engage in quite oddball experiments in lucid dreaming. Worsley, for instance, sometimes creates a lucid dream TV set. With it he can control brightness and colour of the lucid dream scene on the screen, and he has learned to put a frame around part of a lucid dream environment and "freeze" it. He has also invented the lucid dream equivalent to an electronic paintbox. The only limits to your experimentation are those set by your imagination and creativity.

Of all lucid dream activities, flying must be the most joyous and liberating. Flying and lucid dreaming are virtually synonymous. The sensation of lucid dream flight is totally realistic, and all researchers agree that it is a true learning process, continuing from one lucid dream to another, just as if you were developing a physical skill. There are many forms of lucid dream flight – superman style with arms stretched out in front, floating, great bounding leaps in slow motion, vertical ascents, and upright through-the-air travel. You can even float backwards.

Because flying is so realistic and space is fully three-dimensional in lucid dreams, it is easy to have initial problems with taking off. You can be as prone to fear of heights and sensations of vertigo as in waking life. If this is a problem, the best way to get started is to stand on a low hill in your dream, or even a lucid dream chair, and jump off, telling yourself that you will float. When you find that you do, your confidence will increase, and you will gradually fly higher and further. Always impress on your mind that you

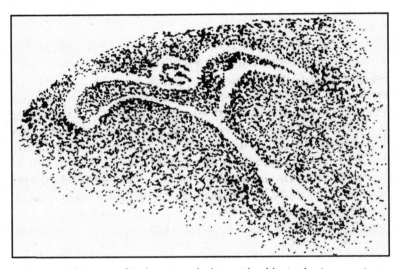

Fig. 13: This piece of rock art is pecked into a boulder in the Amazon, in
territory belonging to a tribe of people who ritually use *ayahuasca*, a powerful
mind-altering concoction that can prompt the sensation of the spirit leaving the
body and flying. Such winged images belonging to shamanic practice
occur worldwide.

cannot harm yourself. There is no need for any fear of flying
in lucid dreams.

Lucid dream flying for Patricia Garfield was often
synonymous with experiencing orgasm. Orgasm in lucid
dreams can be achieved by having sex with a partner of your
choice, or by flying, according to Garfield. She also makes a
telling observation in *Pathway to Ecstasy* that sexual arousal
in lucid dreams can be transformed into a mystic state. She
points out that the use of sexual energy for mystic experience
is what Tantric yogis have done for centuries, releasing the
kundalini energy in the spine. This release of life force, psychic
energy, whatever one calls it, has sexual energy as its physical
manifestation, but it is only a manifestation. If one plumbs

to the centre of what the source energy or force is, one can understand Garfield's claim to be able to mount the waves of the energy to mystic bliss. She says that lucid dreams "are microcosms of the mystic experience". Flight is the very image of ecstasy, and has been used as the metaphor for spirituality from the most primitive shamanic religions to the images of winged angels familiar to us today.

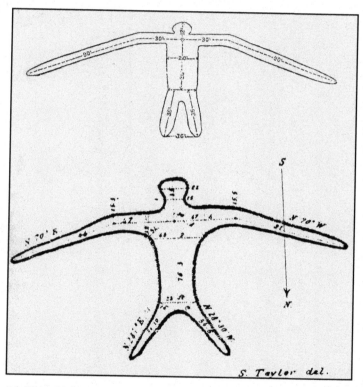

Fig. 14: These 19th-century groundplans are surveys of two huge earthen effigy mounds in the American Upper Midwest, and are examples of many hundreds of such Indian earthworks there. They are a thousand or more years old, and depict a variety of totemic and shamanic images, as is the case here with these human-bird hybrid forms – birds and winged humans being the universal metaphor for spirit flight, which is the experience at the heart of shamanism.

Certainly, a full range of experience is available in lucid dreams. As you become proficient, you can work almost anything out in them, from the most mundane problem to the most exalted personal illumination. Lucid dreaming is as near to total liberation as you will ever attain in this lifetime. It is worth making an effort to achieve it.

CHAPTER 5

THE OUT-OF-BODY EXPERIENCE

O N the rock walls of caves and overhangs in southern Africa, archaeologists have uncovered hundreds of engravings and paintings left by the Bushman (San) people who once inhabited the vast region. These people were hunted to near-extinction by some of the white settlers a century ago, and now only a scatter of descendants of the Bushman still survive, plus a few intact groups in the Kalahari Desert. Bushman rock art can range from hundreds to thousands of years old, and certain images recur in it. One is of a human being, or a human-animal hybrid, with a long line issuing from the top of the head. Until recently, anthropologists and archaeologists disregarded such depictions, assuming their meaning would never be deciphered. But now a group of enterprising archaeological investigators have gone back through the records of what anthropologists learned from the last of the Bushman earlier this century, and have linked that information with interviews with the last-remaining Bushman people. The meaning of much of the rock art imagery has subsequently been deciphered. It was discovered that the lines from the heads of the rock art figures represented a tribally-coded expression of what it felt like to leave one's body through the top of the head during trance dancing, which the Bushman of the Kalahari still practice. It is a prehistoric depiction of the out-of-body experience.

An example of another such prehistoric depiction can be found in a rock shelter half the world away on the Texas-Mexico border. The shelter is festooned with rock paintings four thousand years old; many of them show strange symbols and shapes, but one panel shows a white human-shaped image seemingly rising out of a similar shape that is painted in black. It is widely thought that this image depicts a shaman leaving his body during trance, and because of this the rock shelter is called the White Shaman shelter. Research has shown that the imagery on the rock walls relates to visions had under the influence of the mind-altering cactus, *peyote*. Out-of-body sensations can often occur to people who take this drug.

From antiquity, tribal shamans used bird and arrow symbols to refer to their aerial out-of-body journeys during trance states. Siberian shamans would wear bird-claw shoes, or hang an iron version of a bird's skeleton around their necks. Even in the twenty-thousand-year-old Palaeolithic cave paintings in the cave of Lascaux, France, we can find the depiction of a man in trance wearing a bird-mask near a stick with a bird carved on one end – a symbol of the shaman in Siberia as late as the eighteenth century. Other Siberian shamans would hold arrows point uppermost when performing their trance dance, while another might shoot an arrow from a ritual bow to show tribal members how his spirit could fly from his body. Native American shamans would hang eagle-claw designs cut out of mica on their ceremonial robes, or wear bird-costumes. In South America, a shaman would climb to the top of a pole and flap his or her arms, like wings, symbolising soul-flight.

Fig. 15: Rock art in White Shaman Shelter, Texas. This central panel of the ancient painted images on the rock wall shows a curiously stylised whitish figure (the "white shaman") with tiny outstretched arms and legs seemingly rising out of a similar dark shape. Most researchers consider this to be one of the earliest depictions of the out-of-body experience, the sensation of "spirit flight" at the heart of the shamanic trance. In this case, evidence indicates such a trance state was induced by use of the mind-altering cactus, *peyote*.

Clearly, the out-of-body experience (OBE) has left a deep imprint on the human mind from the remotest times. It is one of the most mysterious events in the experience of humanity, and it cannot be ignored by anyone wanting to know about and practice lucid dreaming.

The model of the OBE that most people know of is that of "astral projection". This idea was brought to the attention of the west through the efforts of Madame Blavatsky and the Theosophical Society in the nineteenth century. The basic idea is that there are seven levels of existence, with physical reality being the densest. The next level is the etheric, which is intermediate between the physical and the third, astral, level. It is the astral body that goes on out-of-body jaunts, though the human being has higher "bodies", vehicles that can operate in the mental, spiritual and higher levels. According to this model, the astral plane is where most of the OBE action takes place.

In the Theosophical teachings, and those of Theosophy's close cousin, Spiritualism, the astral body is supposed to be connected to the physical body by the "silver cord", a kind of elastic, semi-physical or etheric feature.

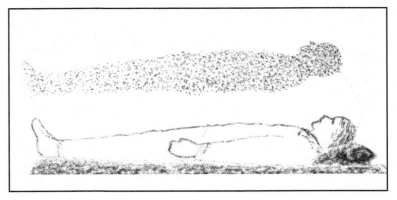

Fig. 16: A classic conception of "astral projection".

Taking Leave of the Body

In an OBE, a person's centre of awareness, the ego or sense of self, seems to float around in free space near the physical body, often above it. A typist saw herself from "about eight feet behind, two feet to the actual left, and four feet above actual height"; a commuter in a train carriage found himself "about ten inches above myself looking down at myself". OBEs can start in a number of ways. Judging from surveys involving hundreds of people conducted by Celia Green in 1966, the majority of cases occur involuntarily. It could be from simple fatigue, as in the case of the waitress who missed her last bus home and had to walk, late at night. She felt exhausted, and had to force herself to press on. "The next I registered," she recalled, "was hearing the sound of my heels very hollowly and I looked down and watched myself walk round the bend ... I remember thinking 'so that's how I look to other people'." More often it happens as a result of an accident or other physical or psychological trauma or stress. A number of OBEs have occurred to rock climbers and mountaineers who slip and fall, and police officers in shoot-outs have reported sensations of becoming disembodied.

Often the person feels that their essence or important part of their self is in the exteriorised location, and view the body with detachment. "Then I saw on my left a group of white-coated figures, bending over 'something' on the floor," one person reported. "Suddenly I realized that that 'something' was me." About a third of Green's respondents had their OBEs while under anaesthetic or while unconscious for some other reason. Many people, though, have OBEs for no apparent reason, such as happened to the person watching a film from the front row of the balcony in a cinema: "All at once I found myself out in space about three feet over the edge of the balcony and I was watching myself sat in the seat."

Sometimes, while having an OBE, a person's physical body can carry on performing its physical activity – walking, driving and so on. Even talking. A number of public speakers have reported that they heard their own voices as if coming from somewhere else, and then found themselves floating over the audience or at the back of the hall watching themselves, still speaking, on the stage, pulpit or podium. It can also take place in socially interactive situations: "It happened always in a noisy, crowded and brightly-lit large room. I would suddenly find myself floating at ceiling level... Below me, I could see myself, talking quite naturally."

Not all OBEs take place during waking life, in arousing, stressful or traumatic situations. A significant category

The physical body can sometimes be seen simply "going through the motions" during an OBE. One of the authors recalls going as a youngster to the swimming baths with a school party. A friend who had never been swimming before was floating around with water up to his chest. His eyes had a glazed look, and he did not respond when spoken to. Later, he explained that after he had jumped in the pool, he suddenly seemed to be up in the roof, watching himself down in the water and being unable to make himself reply to anyone who came up to him. It seems that the shock of being immersed so fully in water with the unfamiliar feeling of buoyancy may have triggered the OBE.

of involuntary OBEs occur when people are falling asleep at night, having a nap, just waking up, or are otherwise in a highly relaxed, quiescent state. "I went to bed early one evening leaving the light on, as I was really only resting... suddenly I sort of 'stepped' out of my body", one person typically remarked. "Lying wide awake in bed one night I had the experience of being lifted into the air with a foot of space between myself and the bed," said another. Usually, though, people awake from sleep to find themselves looking down at their bodies in bed. In some cases, people enter an apparent OBE directly from a lucid dream. In fact, many of the pioneer astral projectionists recommended this as a way of inducing the experience, as they all had experiences that seemed to be lucid dreams in addition to (and associated with) a strand of experience they assumed to involve the literal exteriorisation of the spirit or mind. Oliver Fox called them "Dreams of Knowledge", and Muldoon referred to the process as "Dreaming True".

In her sample, Green found that the physical body was in a lying or sitting posture in over ninety percent of OBEs. She also found that subjects fell into two main groups, those who had just one involuntary experience in their lives, and those who found themselves able to deliberately induce repeated OBEs. Only small numbers had more than one involuntary OBE. Induction was usually performed when falling asleep or waking up. While people who had involuntary OBEs tended to find themselves "out" without knowledge of how they got there, those who induced OBEs were usually conscious of the process of "projection", in which accompanying hissing, roaring, whirring, popping and similar noises, and (non-physical) vibrations are widely reported.

The seeing of one's physical body from "outside" is a general characteristic of the OBE, but doesn't always happen. While in the out-of-body state, people often report finding themselves in an "astral" body which duplicates their physical form. It is usually clothed. Most usually, however, the person is simply aware of being a point of awareness, a sort of disembodied eye, and often simply assumes a body is present without actually noticing anything. Sight seems crisp and stereoscopic, and there is often great mental clarity. (There can be momentary blackouts, especially in induced cases, and temporary foggy vision at the start of an OBE.) There can be sensations of being in two places at once, with feelings from the physical body mixing with OBE sensations. Where not natural, lighting can seem to be generalised, as though not having a source. Sometimes objects can appear to be illuminated from within, and can display a shimmering radiance or energy effect. Some people reporting an OBE have said they were able to see in the dark or pass through solid objects – sometimes with a sense of resistance or texture appropriate to the object being passed through.

The majority of involuntary OBEs take place within a few yards of the physical body – at the scene of the accident, in the operating room, in the bedroom, or whatever the situation is. This is fairly true of induced OBEs too, though the more experienced OBE practitioner will often explore the house, or float out into the neighbourhood, or even venture farther afield while in an "exteriorised" state. This is especially the case when the person wishes to visit someone. Occasionally, experimental journeys have been made during OBEs to distant locales and even into outer space, though only a relatively small percentage of reports involve non-Earth locations, which are sometimes interpreted as astral heavens or hells, or other dimensions or planets.

Those who feel they have been out of their bodies report a variety of ways of returning to the physical form. They may suddenly just find themselves back inside it, or they can return "as quick as lightning". Sometimes the "exteriorised" person just lies down on the physical body to reintegrate, and simply will themselves to return. Occasionally, "re-entry" can be a rough-and-tumble, violent sensation of being vigorously dragged down into the physical body. In a few cases, especially when people go on extended OBEs and seemingly visit locations quite a distance from the physical body, some difficulty in returning to it can be experienced. This can cause fear, anxiety and downright panic. But it seems that reintegration is eventually inevitable, even if such hitches arise. When they again feel themselves to be in their physical bodies, OBE experients find themselves suffering a form of paralysis, sometimes referred to as "astral catalepsy". Movement comes back gradually, often a finger or a toe at a time. Paralysis can also accompany the onset of the OBE, especially when it is being induced, or occurring spontaneously from sleep or a near-sleep condition.

THE NATURE OF THE BEAST

Anyone involved with lucid dreaming has to ask if the OBE is a form of lucid dream. Although there are differences, there are some striking similarities.

Opinion is mixed. Some lucid dreamers and researchers are not sure they are one and the same phenomenon. Patricia

Garfield, for instance, began to have experiences she found to be "truly shocking". "I found myself being projected out of my body in the dream state, will it or not," she confided in *Pathways to Ecstasy*. In a half-asleep state she would feel vibrations and a "tingling-buzz" accompanied by a "whooshing-whirring sound". After some moments of resistance, she felt her "second self" lift up and out of her physical body. She began by simply hovering in the bedroom, but eventually went on various adventures, none of them pleasant. She found her exteriorised self could pass through objects. In one case, it was a graffiti-covered wall. She pushed her hands against it and pushed gently. They passed directly through the wall. She felt a grainy texture, and the graffiti showed clearly through her hands. When she started to pass through a window she felt as if she was suffocating before she broke through. Garfield remained open as to whether such experiences were actual visits to the astral plane or the results of self-induced trance. But she noted she had experiences in the OBEs such as choking sensations and of being "lost" that did not occur in her lucid dreams. She decided to treat the OBE as a logical extension of lucid dreaming – "another level of the unknown".

In 1988, psychologist Harvey Irwin conducted a serious comparative study of lucid dreaming and the OBE. He discovered that the data available did show a statistical link, but that it was fairly weak. Functionally, he noted that Muldoon, Fox and some other astral projectionists had claimed that dream lucidity could be employed as a vehicle for the OBE, but it nevertheless wasn't that easy to quantify an equivalence between the two types of experience. He then checked out what little work had been done on measuring the brain patterns involved in the two phenomena. Some alpha wave activity was noted in OBEs, but little or no REM, which is of course different to most lucid dreams (except those occurring in the hypnogogic stage, where, interestingly, many induced OBEs take place). Overall, the data were too weak to show any links, and Irwin called for more research. He also correlated studies showing the personality types of those who reported lucid dreams and OBEs. Here there were intriguing distinguishing characteristics: there was a tendency in people who had OBEs to be susceptible to migraine attacks, and to be able to absorb themselves in a subject to the exclusion of the world around them, while lucid dreamers specifically did not show these traits. But people having OBEs tended to have their experiences after days of high cortical arousal, as we have noticed earlier with lucid dreaming. So Irwin saw some link between lucid dreaming and those OBEs arising out of stress.

For the early astral travellers and many more recent out-of-body practitioners the OBE was a straightforward matter. They simply assumed that it was literally true that the mind or spirit temporarily leaves the body.

Oliver Fox was born in 1885, and suffered from much illness as a child. He regularly had nightmares, and this forced him to teach himself dream control. He had his first lucid dream when he was a young science student. As he progressed in these "dreams of knowledge", he had one in which he was walking along a beach while having had a dual impression of lying in bed at home. As he deliberately prolonged this lucid dream, Fox heard a "click" in his head, which he associated with the mysterious pineal gland deep in the brain, and the consciousness of his physical body disappeared, leaving him to roam freely. When he got back to his body later, however, he awoke in a cataleptic condition. He eventually learned that this condition can be dissipated by falling back to sleep again after "re-entry". As he continued to experiment, he began to experience "false awakenings". (As we have noted, a false awakening is a dream of waking up in your bedroom, or where ever you went to sleep, that is as realistic as in waking life but where you are unaware that you are dreaming.) He found that by willing his body to move while in this state, he could "project". It was as if his spirit obeyed his will while his physical body was incapacitated. He later discovered that he could project from the waking state: while resting, he found he could enter a trance-like state without falling to sleep first, and the sign he had achieved this was being able to see through closed eyelids. While in that state he learned to exit his body by forcing his attention through the "pineal door" as he called it.

Fox visited locales that were recognisable as being Earth-like, and also a "summerland" type of landscape which he took to be on the astral plane. He had some interactions with

The pineal gland is a small conical structure in the old area of the brain, situated over the brain stem. Its function is not fully understood, though it is known to secrete hormones and has a role in pigmentation in some species. Descartes thought it was the seat of the soul, and some parapsychologists, like Serena-Roney Dougal, think it may produce chemicals similar to those found in some psychoactive plants, such as are found in the hallucinogenic *ayahuasca* mixture used sacramentally by certain Amazonian Indian tribes.

friends while in the out-of-body state, some of which were later apparently verifiable. His means of location while in the astral body was by horizontally gliding, levitation and what he called "skrying", which was a rocket-like vertical ascent. He made only a few mentions of an elastic, cord-like feature linking the astral and physical bodies.

Sylvan Muldoon was another influential astral traveller, as a result of his books with Hereward Carrington. Muldoon was prone to illness, and he makes some ambiguous statements that could be interpreted to mean that he suffered from epilepsy. His first OBE occurred when he was twelve years old, after he had awoken in a state of paralysis, which he would later call "astral catalepsy", and suffering unusual vibrations and heavy pressure in the back of the head. He soon found himself floating in the room. He went on to have a great many OBEs. He tended to refer to his double or astral body as the "phantom", and paid much attention to the cord that connected it with the physical body and along which travelled "pull and push" sensations. He was sure that when it exteriorised the phantom was also cataleptic like the physical body, and this enabled it to move out from the body upwards and then horizontally along. At a certain distance from the physical body (or the "shell" as Muldoon often referred to it) the phantom floated upright and the catalepsy dissolved.

Muldoon reckoned that when we sleep the phantom is slightly out of coincidence with the physical form, and that it normally slips out of the body during the hypnogogic stage. He suggested that dreaming of "aviation"-type actions that emulated the movements of the phantom during sleep could facilitate projection. This was "dreaming true". Also repressing habits and other "activation factors" could lead to a build up of psychological stress that would lead the phantom to move out of the sleeping physical body. Muldoon felt that sexual desire hindered projection.

In more recent times, one of the most prominent OBE proponents was the late Robert Monroe. He was not an occultist but a successful media businessman. While resting one Sunday afternoon in 1958, he experienced strong vibrations. He had several more of these shaking attacks, yet could see no physical movement. He was initially concerned that he was becoming ill, but, reassured that nothing was wrong, he found the courage to remain calm when these symptoms next occurred. His arm was hanging over the side of the bed, and he suddenly found he could feel his way through the floorboards. On a later occasion, the vibrations returned when he was thinking about going gliding. He suddenly found himself bouncing against the ceiling.

Monroe eventually learned how to consciously induce OBEs, and became proficient in the experience. He categorised three basic types of out-of-body environments he called "locales":

- **Locale I:** essentially the here and now – Earth scenes.
- **Locale II:** a non-material realm of thought which has inhabitants and an unpleasant region at its "closest" to the physical world.
- **Locale III:** first experienced as a black hole through a wall by Monroe, this transpired to be a sort of parallel dimension in which earth-like scenes were to be found, but where the history and technology were unfamiliar.

Monroe travelled in the out-of-body state by concentrating on a destination and then stretching out the upper body and arms and "pushing" in the desired direction. Contradictory to Muldoon, he considered the sex drive to be a useful factor, and found that by diverting it to other bodily areas he could trigger the vibration state. (This happens to have been similar to the application of the sex drive as practiced by Tantric dream yogis.) Monroe sometimes noted the presence of a cord, but did not make an issue of it. He encountered both human and non-human entities. He set up an institute to investigate and promote ways of entering the out-of-body state (www.monroeinstitute.org).

Fox, Muldoon and Monroe all mentioned the presence of "currents" or "astral winds" in the out-of-body state that could whisk the OBE experient off course to unexpected locations. Interestingly, Monroe ascribed this to an undisciplined mental state rather than actual other-worldly environmental effects.

Another relatively recent out-of-body practitioner is Keith Harary. While he has been able to enter the out-of-body state since childhood, he is also a parapsychologist who scientifically investigates apparent paranormal phenomena. He considers lucid dreaming and the OBE to be both psychologically and physiologically distinct, though does not necessarily argue that anything actually "leaves" the physical body during an OBE. He feels that no one knows what the OBE really is. In one experiment carried out at Duke University, Harary used randomly-timed OBEs to "visit" his pet cat at a remote location. The monitored animal showed significantly quieter behaviour when Harary was "with" it. This contrasts somewhat with vain attempts made by Muldoon half a century earlier to get his pet dog to respond to his "phantom".

There are other researchers who are pretty sure that lucid dreams and OBEs are versions of the same basic mental phenomenon. They see some fundamental psychophysiological core with subjective elements added. Paul Tholey's laboratory research in Germany indicated similarities between lucid dreams and at least some kinds of OBEs. British psychologist Sue Blackmore notes that all those claiming an OBE provide differing accounts, especially with regard to what they see while "out". She had a protracted OBE herself, in which she floated up through a ceiling and out above the rooftops of Oxford. Later she checked the colour of the tiles and other details on the roof of the building where she had her experience, and found some distinct differences to what she had seen in her OBE.

What Leaves the Body?

Blackmore feels that many people having an OBE think that their out-of-body surroundings are convincingly real, but rarely actually bother to check details. She suggests that both lucid dreams and the OBE are simply different models of the world supplied by the brain when normal sensory channels are cut off by sleep, trauma, drugs, anaesthetic, sensory deprivation, trance (which can include states of fatigue, hypnogogia or even aimless lack of attention), and so forth. Many people have difficulty with this explanation because of the powerful realism both lucid dreaming and the OBE can display. A moment's thought, however, is sufficient to make us realise that if the brain-mind can produce the realism of a lucid dream, the apparent realism of an OBE is hardly a different matter.

We rarely consider the slightly uncomfortable fact that we all inhabit a mental world all the time. We never see even the physical world as it is: its description by physicists is not what we experience in our daily lives. We have no idea what a tree, a house, a mountain, or a loved one really is. Our sense organs transduce energies like light and sound waves that impinge upon them from the outer physical world into electrochemical signals that are processed in fabulously complex ways within the brain. The sunrise that greets our eyes is produced entirely in the darkness of our skulls, not by light leaking into our heads as it might penetrate a camera. At the same time, our brains map an image of our bodies, and process bodily (somatic) signals. Space as we experience it is an information-ordering device conjured up by the brain-mind (the mind is the subjective "interior" of the physically objective brain).

So the world around us, our physical body and its placing within the environment all result from mental models constantly and furiously updated by our brain-minds. In a traumatic situation, like a car accident, in sleep and trance, in mental illness or under sensory deprivation conditions or the influence of drugs or anaesthetic, this carefully-constructed model can become distorted, and the sense of time, space and body image can alter drastically. The sense of self, the ego, can change its apparent location inside the head and move to different parts of the body or even outside it altogether.

The ego itself is a mirage, a focusing of mental processes much like the two images in a stereoscope coalesce into one 3D image. You may think "you" are there somewhere behind the forehead, just above and between the eyebrows, but in truth there is nothing there other than bone and tissue. There is no little person inside your head looking out through the windows and doors of the sense organs at the big wide world outside. That is an illusion. So as we are not in our bodies, the question of an OBE cannot really arise – what is there to leave the body?

According to people like Blackmore, what is happening is that the mental model is being altered; without information coming through the normal sensory channels in the usual way, the brain-mind uses its model-making processes to conjure up what it can from the information available – largely from sources in memory. To you the result looks just as real as it does in everyday waking reality. If your ego is impaired, as in a normal dream or a fever, you take the model for reality. If your sense of self is intact, but a hallucination occurs unexpectedly, as in, for example, an OBE, you can still think the brain-mind production is the real thing. In a lucid dream, self –awareness is also present, but you are lucid enough to recognise that you are within a dream, a mental construct. In such a view, the only essential difference between an OBE and a lucid dream is that in the latter you know what is actually happening, however realistic the surroundings may seem, while in the former you believe you are experiencing real events.

To some extent this approach to the OBE has been supported by various kinds of laboratory experiments in the first decade of the twenty-first century. One has involved the electrical stimulation of parts of the brain repeatedly triggering OBEs. Another range of trials has involved subjects wearing goggles showing a live video image of their own back. This can cause a confusion of sensory information causing a cognitive displacement regarding the mind's usual body-image mapping that can in turn promote a sense of disassociation from the body.

NIGHT TERRORS

Stephen Laberge and colleagues such as Lynne Levitan have come to similar conclusions to Blackmore. Their laboratory studies indicated that OBEs showed a distinct link with wake-initiated lucid dreams (WILDS) specifically, and extensive surveys of people concerning their dream-related experiences at home showed an association between OBEs, lucid dreaming, and the phenomenon of sleep paralysis.

Sleep paralysis is well-known to psychologists and dream researchers, and it occurs because a person is waking up from or falling into REM sleep, where most vivid dreams occur. We have noted in an earlier chapter that during REM sleep most muscles in the body apart from the eyes and the respiratory mechanism lose their tone, creating a kind of paralysis so that the dreamer cannot act out the actions of a dream. In sleep paralysis, even though the person has physically awakened, REM brain activity is still continuing. This "out of synch" state can last up to several minutes. The international scientific classification of sleep paralysis is that it is "a period of inability to perform voluntary movements either at sleep onset ... or upon awakening either during the night or in the morning". Separate studies by both Celia Green and Susan Blackmore revealed that over eighty percent of OBEs take place when the physical body is lying down or sitting, and usually when sleeping, dreaming, napping, resting, ill or otherwise incapacitated. All these are conditions in which muscle tone will be much reduced.

Experiences reported in sleep paralysis are remarkably similar to those described by those undergoing the onset of OBEs. People feel "eerie, rushing experiences" and a "roaring in the head". Others have described a "buzzing or/and shuffling sound in the ears", a "sound like a spring uncoiling or a crackle of electricity", and sensations of being touched or pulled, having pressure applied to the body, floating, and vibration. These can be accompanied by voices whispering in the ear or the sense of a presence, often malign, being in the room. Researchers think these sensations may be the hallucinatory embroidering of signals originating in middle ear activity and other internal processes.

The most notorious of sleep paralysis hallucinations is that of the "Old Hag", well described in David Hufford's study of "hagging" experiences reported in his book, *The Terror That Comes in the Night*. A classic case happened to Ronald Siegel, a well-known psychologist at UCLA. He awoke shortly after 4 am and heard footsteps accompanied by heavy breathing approaching his bed. He found he was unable to get up to see what was going on. As the presence got closer, Siegel caught a whiff of a musty odour. He next saw a shadow fall across the bed and felt something touch his neck and arm. A voice whispered in his ear in a strange language, like English spoken backwards. As he heard this, he saw images of rotting vegetation and hideous reptiles. An expert in hallucinations, Siegel suspected that was what it was, but he was nevertheless terrified. From what he could see, with his head turned to one side, the bedroom looked otherwise normal. When a cold, deathly hand started squeezing his arm, Siegel began to doubt a hallucinatory explanation. His fear grew deeper as he felt a weight get on the bed and the mattress give beneath it, causing the bed to creak. He sensed the still-whispering entity to be female and evil, emanating an aura of dark sexuality. The scientist could hardly breathe, as the thing's jelly-like body crushed down onto him. Gradually, the pressure and the paralysis eased, and Siegel was able to move once more. He leapt out of bed and found no one else in the apartment. Recovering from the shock, the psychologist realised he had suffered a bout of sleep paralysis and that he had been having hypnopompic, REM-based hallucinations.

The "Old Hag" and often-reported dark-hooded figures in sleep paralysis episodes seem to be versions of the *incubus* and *succubus* in medieval and earlier times. Siegel showed in the analysis of his experience that a combination of physiological factors, sexual arousal from REM sleep, and the victim's own struggles against paralysis produced a mix of sensations that were synthesised into a complex of hallucinatory effects. Compared to this, the OBE seems quite tame!

FALSE AWAKENINGS

False awakenings can be seemingly as realistic as in real life but you are unaware that you are dreaming. A lucid dream minus the lucidity, in other words – Van Eeden's "wrong-waking-up" dreams. Like nightmares, they can sometimes be accompanied by an anxious or disturbing feeling. Often when he experienced one of his "wrong-waking-up" dreams, Van Eeden noticed them to be illuminated by "a strong diabolical light". LaBerge has described a number of his own false awakenings, some of which he was initially prepared to believe were genuine OBEs, for the surroundings of the bedroom, and seeing his own body sleeping on the bed, seemed completely convincing. But then he would notice some detail about the room that was incorrect, or some dream-like event would intervene. Such factors gave the game away, and he realised he was in a kind of specialised lucid dream.

ENCOUNTERS

Sleep paralysis, false awakenings and strange beings call to mind experiments by that master lucid dreamer, Alan Worsley. He has devised a technique in which he lays down and attempts to enter a lucid dream state directly from waking. He lies dead still for an hour or two at a time in what seems to be a simulated version of sleep paralysis. This can produce what Worsley refers to as "sleep onset lucid dreams". These often commence as non-visual, with tactile, auditory and kinesthetic sensations dominating. In one, he could feel a creature with scaly skin slither over him, and bite him with needle-sharp teeth. In another, he felt himself being operated on by robots. (One can't help but wonder if so-called UFO abductions could be associated with the spontaneous occurrence in a person of a similar mental state. It is noteworthy that many "abduction" experiences commence while the "abductee" is in bed, having a nap, or engaging in trance-inducing activities like driving long distances at night.) Sometimes, someone might seem to enter the room or a cat walk over the bed, the telephone might sound as if it is ringing, or his limbs might feel as if they are moving (even though they are physically immobile). Worsley calls such experiences "haptic dreams". It is very difficult to lie still when such disturbing events are apparently taking place, but Worsley has found that if he can remain calm the lucid dream proceeds, and visual elements finally kick in. This becomes such a powerful experience that Worsley calls them "superlucid" dreams. "They seem to be comparable to out-of-the-body experiences," he says, "yet I interpret them as dreams, not as out-of-the-body experiences."

In the final analysis, you, the reader, will have to make up your own mind as to the real nature of the OBE. We have deliberately given you enough information from both sides of the argument as to whether OBEs are a form of lucid dream. We suggest the following somewhat simplified "spectrum" might be the actual situation, with shades in between:

Lucid Dream → *Sleep Paralysis* → *OBE* → *False Awakening*

In such a view, lucid dreaming is one of a closely-related set of contiguous mental states. But, select what model feels comfortable for you. If you decide to treat OBEs as being literally the exteriorisation of the mind or spirit from the physical body, then proceed with caution, and explore the range of techniques given below. We simply advise that you be fully aware that they can result in experiences that are not necessarily so pleasant as lucid dreams.

Outward Bound

The techniques used for inducing OBEs are essentially similar to lucid dream inductions, but with a different emphasis. The power of place (spatial programming) takes on special importance, and ways of developing a dual awareness can be helpful. Most OBE practitioners agree that when inducing the experience, physical relaxation is most important. A state of relaxed alertness is the ideal to be sought.

There seems to be no special dietary advice for OBE induction, though Muldoon recommended fasting and a reduction in the taking of liquids on days when induction is being attempted. On the other hand, Garfield found that she had her strongest (and most frightening) OBE when she had been "inordinately stuffed with food"! As far as posture is concerned, there are likewise no universal rules. Muldoon felt that sleeping on one's back was best, and failing that, the right side. Garfield felt that lying on one's back or left side best facilitated OBEs. Monroe said that the aspiring OBE practitioner should lie with his or her head towards the north, but Garfield argued that it made no difference what direction one slept in. Perhaps the only golden rule is to simply experiment! You have to find what works for you.

Select from the following methods, which have been laid out in an order with developmental exercises first, then actual induction techniques following. Put these in the context of the skills and approaches you have learned from your dream and lucid dream work where appropriate, so you can devise your own elaborations around the core concepts offered here, if you so wish. These exercises and techniques derive from traditional methods as well as suggestions from workers in OBE and lucid dream research. We have also presented some new ones, based on sound principles. Remember that many of the techniques described as being for use at sleep onset can also be used equally well (and often even better) on re-entering sleep after waking up in the morning. As with the lucid dream methods in Chapter 4, some of the techniques described here will work well together, others will not and are alternatives. Pick and choose as you wish, remembering that all such exercises often require the investment of time and effort to bring results.

Remember Me

Observe yourself in the day – we tend to do things in a merely semi-conscious haze most of the time. Try to "catch" yourself putting on your shoes in the morning, reaching for the phone, walking down the street, driving your car. Such "self-remembering" develops a kind of dual consciousness of observer and observed that can be extremely appropriate for OBE induction practices.

Who am I?

This is a variation on the above method. One of Celia Green's correspondents found it possible to induce a sense of floating a foot or two out of the body when walking alone on a deserted road, travelling in a bus, or in bed at night by saying inwardly "What am I? Who am I?" repeatedly.

Air Time

This is perhaps the simplest and most fun of all developmental exercises for OBEs. On the day when you want to induce an OBE, spend a good couple of hours with a kite, in the park or countryside. Feel the tug of the kite on the line, its soaring and gliding on the air currents or in the breeze. Preferably use one of those kites you can control, so you can make it swoop and dive. Identify with the kite as you feel its movements on the string. Imagine yourself up there, gliding, soaring, floating. Really get into it. That night in bed, after you have performed an incubation for an OBE and done your relaxation exercises, drift off towards the hypnogogic stage while recalling your kite session. See it in your mind's eye swooping through the sky, and imagine the feeling of being the kite.

If you practice hang-gliding or para-gliding, then this exercise can, of course, be made even more graphic, as you will actually be able to recall your motion in the air.

Water Baby

This challenges the above for being the number one fun exercise. Float on a water bed or rubber rings in a swimming pool, with your eyes closed. Feel the floating sensation. Imagine you are out-of-your body. Absorb the physical sensation into your memory. Mentally replay it when floating away to sleep that night.

Taken for a Ride

Another of Celia Green's subjects had an OBE while travelling on a bus. The person spent a great deal of time afterwards trying to figure out how and why it happened. "I know when I first got on the bus of thinking to myself that I am inclined to tense myself up to meet situations which are in front of me," the person said. "I insisted to myself that I make an effort to relax – and instead of travelling *with* the bus I let the bus *take* me." A subtle but crucial shift of emphasis is being pointed out here. It is really a focus for letting go. Literally a vehicle for deep relaxation in a situation where an undercurrent of tension is usually present. Try it when you are a passenger in a car, or on a bus, train or aircraft. It is a delicious feeling that just happens to put you in the right mental and physical state for an OBE. *Bon voyage!*

Laid Back

Most OBE experts state that physical relaxation is an important factor in any induction of an OBE (as distinct from stress-related involuntary ones in active waking life). So when you go to bed at night intending to have an OBE, or a lucid dream, undergo a relaxation exercise that systematically releases the tension in all your main muscle groups from head to toe. You can choose your own method, or one you may have learned elsewhere, as long as you consciously work your way up through your entire body deliberately relaxing the muscles as you go, especially the facial muscle groups around the eyes and the mouth, and especially the tongue. If done properly, the entire exercise should take about fifteen minutes, or even longer.

Mirror, Mirror on the Wall

How often do you see the back of your head? It is a startling fact that only a minority of people have seen their own spine. Let's put that right. Find some quiet, private time. Undress. Using a large wall mirror and a hand mirror in combination, look at yourself naked from the front, from the sides, and from the rear. Slowly. Completely. In detail. Get to know your body from all sides. Pay special attention to the rear view – the back of the head and neck, the spine.

That night (or immediately after your session with the mirrors), perform your induction and relaxation exercise, and drift off to sleep. As you do so, picture clearly in your mind your body image from all angles. Especially that rear view. Keep these images before you as you sink into the hypnogogic stage.

As indicated above, more technological versions of this exercise are being used in laboratory experiments, where video cameras take the place of mirrors. In one exercise, the subject sits staring at the projected live video image of his back.

On the Record

With a mobile phone or other device, digitally record the ambient sounds at some place familiar to you – a city square, a park bench, a waterfall, or wherever. While making the recording (for several minutes or as long as your device allows), look around and make a special effort to absorb your visual impressions of the place. At night, after your usual incubation and relaxation procedures, close the light and play the sounds you recorded, imagining yourself back at that location as you drift off to sleep. Tell yourself that you want to go there tonight.

Here and There

There are simpler ways of using place as a tool. For instance, Oliver Fox suggested that when you are in the drowsy, hypnogogic state, visualise some street or country track well known to you, and imagine yourself walking along it, noting the buildings, trees and other details on either side as you pass. Fox reckoned that though the mental image may seem to be at an indeterminate distance in front of your closed eyes, you will nevertheless know that the scene is within you. What you are attempting to do is to transfer your consciousness to the chosen locality so that you become within the scene, just as when you actually walk down the road or path in waking life.

Fox touched on some deep perceptual mechanisms here, and you need to think about this as you continue to walk the scene in your mind. When you succeed in making the transfer, Fox promised it will happen instantaneously (in his case, it was accompanied by a mental "click"). "It is, indeed, a very strange sensation, as that which was previously internal (being contained within your mind) suddenly becomes external and contains you," Fox commented. He referred to this method as "instantaneous projection".

Sylvan Muldoon similarly observed that the "phantom" projects more easily to a familiar place. He recommended that when sleeping away from home in a strange setting like a hotel, you should will your mind back to your usual bed as you fall asleep.

You can even use the spatial-memory effect of place in your own home. Before retiring for the night, physically walk to another room from your bed. Go to the front door or to a window and be conscious of every inch of the way. Imagine you are having an OBE. Do the journey several times in close repetition. Absorb every detail of the short journey. Shortly afterwards, as you fall asleep, imagine you are making that journey again. Keep repeating it into sleep.

Working Up a Thirst

Muldoon claimed that desire, habit and the repression of habitually performed actions could all cause astral projection in their different ways. One (rather harsh) exercise he found successful himself was to instil a thirst, hence a desire to drink, prior to going to sleep. On the day of the OBE attempt, severely limit your intake of liquids (but do not refrain from drinking entirely, or try this method if you have medical reasons for taking in liquids). It is especially effective to deprive yourself of a drink in the morning, and to take only occasional sips of water through the day. Intensify your desire to drink by deliberately bringing a tumbler of water to your lips at various times in the day, but not drinking from it. Look at a glass of water. Gaze at it. Concentrate on the water, but don't drink it. Before retiring at night, take a few sips of salted water. Leave a tall glass of clear, cool sparkling water out on a kitchen surface before you go to bed. Walk back to the glass from your bed, as if you were having an OBE, effectively repeating the previous exercise. Do not drink from the glass, but every time you reach it tell yourself that you are out of your body. Repeat this process physically several times, then mentally repeat it as you slip into sleep.

Framed

When in bed, relaxed and preparing to fall asleep, keep your eyes open and use the forefinger and thumb of each hand stretched out into arcs and brought up to your face so as to frame the edges of your field of vision. Then hold the hands in these relative positions as you move them both away from your face. You'll see they form a rough circle about five-to-eight inches across. You have given a physical dimension to a phenomenological aspect of yourself known as "the Cyclop's eye": you see that other people have two eyes, but you yourself feel that you see with one eye almost as big as your face, like the visor on an astronaut's space helmet. Look at the circle formed by your fingers and thumbs, and imagine it as a sphere, glowing softly like the moon, floating just above your face. Close your eyes, keeping that image as you fall asleep.

Face to Face

This exercise is the "outer" version of the inner or phenomenological one just described. It is particularly useful if you are not too good at strong visualisation. Hold a hand mirror over your face as you lie in bed. See your own face looking down at you. Close your eyes, lower the mirror. Visualise your face hovering above you (actually, you only have to remember it doing so). Open your eyes, raise the mirror, and repeat. Carry this out as many times as you can until you are so tired you are ready to fall asleep. You will know when this is as you will start to drop the mirror as you wink off to sleep, acting as a signal in the same way as your falling forearm does in other hypnogogic exercises. Let yourself fall asleep, with that face hovering in front of your mind's eye...

Space Walk

Lie in bed, after your induction and relaxation procedures. Close your eyes, and imagine yourself as a small bead-sized ball of light inside your head, behind and slightly above your eyes. Imagine you, your self or ego, as this ball of light floating inside your body much as you might be inside a big, bulky space suit. When you have got used to this sensation, let the small ball of light grow until it is the same size as your skull. Hold it there for a short time, then let it carry on expanding as a luminous sphere outside of your head. Keep identifying with this sphere as it gradually expands. Feel it and your spectral self grow and grow until it/you is touching the ceiling and perhaps the walls. Stop expanding at this point, and hold the visualisation and the sense of being expanded beyond your body. Hold it for as long as you can manage as you descend into the hypnogogic state.

Leaving Without You

In a 1983 paper, Paul Tholey observed that if you concentrate on your body as you fall asleep "it often happens that the body begins to become immobile". Whether this happens or not, as you fall asleep think of your physical body, become vividly aware of its posture and position. Keep this in mind while mentally changing the position of your body – superimpose a differently-positioned body image. Do not physically move. Try out some specific mental postures. Muldoon thought simply of rising into the air. Or, sink down into and through the bed. Or, again, imagine your body sitting up in bed, letting its legs and feet sink through the bed to the floor, standing up and walking over to the bedroom door. Yet again, give what Monroe called "peel-off" a try: imagine slowly rolling over sideways, leaving the physical body behind, and lying prone next to it.

This mental changing of your body image's position can work with or without sleep paralysis. But should you find yourself "fixed" into immobility, either as you are falling asleep or if you awake from sleep and find yourself in that condition, and can keep cool enough, the practice of this induction will almost always be successful. Try it, too, first thing when you awake naturally in the morning, before you have opened your eyes and physically moved your body position.

I Ain't Got No Body

An alternative approach is to imagine you have no body at all. Tholey called it the "ego-point technique" and it is an advanced method. Consider that when you fall asleep you are no longer conscious of your body. When you dream you may have a dream-body, but that is merely a convention. You are actually just a point of awareness, like the bead of light in "Space walk", above. Being aware of that, imagine yourself as a pinhead of awareness as you observe the flashes of hypnogogic imagery. Focus on this imagery. You feel your body dissolving, and you are just that point of consciousness. Just before you enter sleep, let that ego-point of awareness float off into the hypnogogic imagery, free and easy, like the floating seed from a dandelion. Hold to that point of awareness. Stay with it. If you do so, the hypnogogic imagery will cease, and you can float freely away into a space that seems identical to your bedroom.

As we say, this is an advanced technique, as it requires keeping aware well into the hypnogogic state. You will need proficiency in the exercises in "Entering the Twilight Zone" in Chapter 4 before attempting this.

Going Up

It has already been discussed that it is possible to have an OBE directly from a dream or lucid dream. To help promote this situation, it is useful to incubate a suitable dream. The classic one is a flying dream of some kind. Muldoon, we recall, likewise advised dreaming of "aviation" subjects: flying like a bird, going up in a balloon, piloting an aircraft, swinging in a seat on a rising Ferris wheel. He also felt that dreams of rising upward in an elevator could trigger an OBE. He suggested an incubation in which you lie on your back prior to sleep, and imagine you are lying on the floor of an elevator. You are going to lie there quietly and go to sleep. As you enter sleep the elevator is going to move upwards. You will even feel it trembling slightly as it rises to the top floor. When the lift feels as if it stops, mentally sit up, then stand up and walk out onto the top floor. You will walk round up there, and look out of the windows, and see how high you are. Muldoon felt that this scenario mimicked the motions of the phantom as it left the body during sleep.

Using the False Awakening

If you find yourself in a lucid dream, remember that an easy way to provoke a false awakening is to cover your dream-body's eyes with its hands, while thinking of your bedroom. If you achieve a false awakening, and can control it, it is but a short step to having an OBE. The trouble is, although you have retained the visual clarity of a lucid dream, you have lost a lot of your critical awareness, and think what you see is really your bedroom. The only real way to prepare for this situation is to reality-test every morning when you wake up, then the habit should follow in a false awakening. Is everything in place, as you left it? Is the view out of the window normal? If you have a digital clock, check it once, look away, check it again – do the figures behave in a stable fashion? If the answer is "no" to any or all of these, you may be experiencing a false awakening. (If you do not have a digital clock, then arrange to have some writing visible from your bed.)

Oliver Fox used two guidelines: he knew he was having a false awakening if he could sense a definite feeling of rigidity in his body, and if there was what he called a "sense of strain" in the atmosphere, like that "before the storm" feeling, only more so. When you have the cues that you are in this situation, try to sit up out of your body, ignoring any sounds, flashes of imagery or other distractions that may occur. "Just swing your (astral) legs to the floor and stand up," he advised. "You will then experience dual consciousness." By this, he meant you feel yourself lying in bed and standing up at the same time. This sensation will decrease as you move further away from the bed. You may or may not see your recumbent form on your bed.

You are having an OBE. Are you really out of your body, or are you having a specific form of lucid dream? You decide.

SELECT BIBLIOGRAPHY

Blackmore, Susan, (1982), *Beyond the Body*. Paladin (1983 edn.), Granada Publishing, London.

Blackmore, Susan, (1988), "A Theory of Lucid Dreams and OBEs", in Gackenbach and LaBerge, eds., op cit.

Blackmore, Susan, (1990), "Dreams That Do What They're Told", *New Scientist*, 6 January.

Cartwright, Rosalind Dymond, (1978), *A Primer on Sleep and Dreaming*. Addison-Wesley, Reading, Massachusetts.

Colt, George Howe, (1995), "The Power of Dreams", *Life*, September.

Delaney, Gayle, (1995), *The Dream Kit*. HarperCollins, San Francisco.

Devereux, Charla, (1993), *The Aromatherapy Kit*. Headline, London.

Devereux, Paul, (1996), *Re-Visioning the Earth*. Simon & Schuster, New York.

Devereux, Paul, (2010), *Sacred Geography*. Gaia (Octopus), London.

Fontana, David, (1994), *The Secret Language of Dreams*. Pavilion Books, London.

Fox, Oliver, (undated), "Astral Projection, Course G/01". Archer's Court, Hastings, UK

Freud, Sigmund, (1900), *The Interpretation of Dreams*. Avon Books (1965 edn.), New York.

Gackenbach, Jayne, and LaBerge, Stephen, eds., (1988), *Conscious Mind, Sleeping Brain*. Plenum Press, New York.

Garfield, Patricia, (1974), *Creative Dreaming*. Simon and Schuster, New York.

Garfield, Patricia, (1979), *Pathway to Ecstasy*. Holt, Rinehart and Winston, New York.

Gillespie, George, (1988), "Lucid Dreams in Tibetan Buddhism", in Gackenbach and LaBerge, eds., op cit.

Green, Celia, (1968), *Lucid Dreams.* Institute of Psychophysical Research, Oxford.

Green, Celia, (1968), *Out-of-the-Body Experiences.* Institute of Psychophysical Research, Oxford.

Halliday, Gordon, (1988), "Lucid Dreaming: Using Nightmares and Sleep-Wake Confusion", in Gackenbach and LaBerge, eds., op cit.

Harary, Keith, and Weintraub, Pamela, (1990), *Have an Out of Body Experience in 30 Days.* Aquarian Press, Wellingborough, UK.

Harary, Keith, and Weintraub, Pamela, (1989), *Lucid Dreams in 30 Days.* Aquarian Press, Wellingborough, UK.

Hearne, Keith, (1990), *The Dream Machine.* Aquarian Press, Wellingborough, UK.

Hersh, James, (1979), "Ancient Celtic Incubation", *Sundance Community Dream Journal,* Winter.

Hobson, J. Allan, (1988), *The Dreaming Brain.* Basic Books, HarperCollins, USA.

Hobson, J. Allan, (1994), *The Chemistry of Conscious States.* Little, Brown, Boston.

Hufford, David J., (1982). *The Terror That Comes in the Night.* University of Pennsylvania Press, Philadelphia.

Irwin, Harvey J., (1988), "Out-of-the-Body Experiences and Dream Lucidity: Empirical Perspectives", in Gackenbach and LaBerge, eds., op cit

Kasas, Savas, and Struckmann, Reinhard, (1990), *Important Medical Centres in Antiquity.* Editions Kasas, Athens.

Kay, A.S., (1996), "Psychedelics and Lucid Dreaming: Doorways in the Mind", *Towards 2012,* Part II, July.

Kelzer, Kenneth, (1987), *The Sun and the Shadow.* ARE Press, Virginia Beach.

Krippner, Stanley, ed., (1990), *Dreamtime & Dreamwork.* Jeremy Tarcher, Los Angeles.

LaBerge, Stephen, (1985), *Lucid Dreaming.* Ballantine Books (1986 edn.), New York.

LaBerge, Stephen, Phillips, Leslie, and Levitan, Lynne, (1994), "An Hour of Wakefulness Before Morning Naps Makes Lucidity More Likely", *NightLight,* vol.6, no.3.

LaBerge, Stephen, and Phillips, Leslie, (1994), "Word Association Tests and Brain Functioning in Waking and Dreaming", *NightLight,* vol.6, no.4

LaBerge, Stephen, and Rheingold, Howard, (1990), *Exploring the World of Lucid Dreaming.* Ballantine Books (1991 edn.), New York.

Lang, Mabel, (1977), *Cure and Cult in Ancient Corinth.* Corinth Notes No.1, American School of Classical Studies at Athens, Princeton.

Laughlin, Charles D., McManus, John, and d'Aquili, Eugene G., (1990), *Brain, Symbol and Experience.* Columbia University Press (1992 edn.), New York.

Laughlin, Charles D., (2011), "Communing with the Gods: The Dreaming Brain in Cross-Cultural Perspective", *Time & Mind* vol.4, no.2, July.

Levitan, Lynne, and LaBerge, Stephen, (1991), "Other Worlds: Out-of-Body Experiences and Lucid Dreams", *NightLight,* vol.3, nos.2, 3.

Lewis-Williams, J.D., and Dowson, T.A., (1988), "The Signs of All Times", *Current Anthropology,* 29, no.2.

Mavromatis, Andreas, (1987), *Hypnagogia.* Routlege & Kegan Paul (1991 edn.), London.

MacDonald, George F., Cove, John, Laughlin, Charles, and McManus, John, (1989), "Mirrors, Portals, and Multiple Realities", *Zygon,* vol.24, no.1.

Monroe, Robert, A., (1972), *Journeys out of the Body.* Souvenir Press (1996 edn.), London

Muldoon, Sylvan, J., and Carrington, Hereward, (1929), *The Projection of the Astral Body.* Rider and Company (1965 edn.), London.

Nerys, Dee, (1989), *The Dreamer's Workbook.* The Aquarian Press, Wellingborough, UK.

Parker, Julia and Derek, (1985), *Dreaming*. Mitchell Beazley (1986 edn.), London.

Price, Robert F., and Cohen, David B., (1988), "Lucid Dream Induction: An Empirical Evaluation", in Gackenbach and LaBerge, eds., op cit.

Reed, Henry, (1976), "Dream Incubation: A Reconstruction of a Ritual in Contemporary Form", *Journal of Humanistic Psychology*, vol.16, no.4.

Roney-Dougal, Serena (2010), *Where Science and Magic Meet*. Green Magic, London. Stathe, UK. (There are several earlier editions of this title.)

Rose, Nicholas, Hogan, Jennie, and Blackmore, Susan, (1997), "Experiences of Sleep Paralysis", *Proceedings of Papers Presented at the 40th Annual Convention,* The Parapsychological Association and the Society for Psychical Research.

Siegel, Ronald K., and West, L.J., eds., (1975), *Hallucinations*. John Wiley, New York.

Siegel, Ronald K., (1992), *Fire in the Brain*. Plume (1993 edn.), Penguin, New York.

Targ, Russell, and Harary, Keith, (1984), *The Mind Race*. Villard Books, New York.

Tart, Charles, ed, (1969), *Altered States of Consciousness*. John Wiley, New York.

Taylor, Jeremy, (1992), "The Healing Spirit of Lucid Dreaming", *Shaman's Drum*, Spring.

Tedlock, Barbara, ed., (1987), *Dreaming*. SAR Press (1992 edn.), Santa Fe.

Tholey, Paul, (1983), "Relation Between Dream Content and Eye Movements Tested by Lucid Dreams", *Perceptual and Motor Skills*, 56.

Tholey, Paul, (1983), "Techniques for Inducing and Manipulating Lucid Dreams", *Perceptual and Motor Skills*, 57.

Tholey, Paul, (1989), "Consciousness and Abilities of Dream Characters Observed During Lucid Dreaming", *Perceptual and Motor Skills*, 68.

Tholey, Paul, (1990), "Applications of Lucid Dreaming in Sports", *Lucidity Letter,* vol.9, no.2.

Tholey, Paul, (1991), "Overview of the Development of Lucid Dream Research in Germany", *Lucidity,* 10.

Ullman, Montague, Krippner, Stanley, and Vaughan, Alan, (1989), *Dream Telepathy.* McFarland, Jefferson, North Carolina.

Ullman, Montague, and Limmer, Claire, (1987), *The Variety of Dream Experience.* Crucible (1989 edn.), Wellingborough, UK.

Van de Castle, Robert L., (1994), *Our Dreaming Mind.* Aquarian/ HarperCollins, London.

Worsley, Alan, (1988), "Personal Experiences in Lucid Dreaming", in Gackenbach and LaBerge, eds., op cit.

INDEX